Hope Again

Finding God's Purpose in your Pain

citylight
CHURCH

Hope Again
© 2017 by Jacob M. Rodriguez

Published by CityLight Publications

ISBN-13: 978-1545409053
ISBN-10: 1545409056

All Scripture quotations, unless otherwise specified, are from the New International Version of the Bible. Copyright © 1973, 1978, 1984, International Bible Society. Scripture quotations marked NKJV are from the New King James Version of the Bible. Copyright © 1979, 1980, 1982 by Thomas Nelson, Inc., publishers. Emphasis within Scripture is the author's own. Please note that the author's writing style is to capitalize certain pronouns in Scripture and text that refer to God, and may differ from other religious publishers' styles.

Published in the United States by CityLight Publications, a ministry of CityLight Church, Mountain View, California.

www.citylightonline.org
www.jacobrodriguez.org

To Makai and Chloe

OTHER BOOKS BY JACOB RODRIGUEZ

The Woman's Touch
The Lord's Lady
La Dama del Señor
Hidden Kings
Someone Like Me
Crave
Shift
Lying Lions
HerStory

CONTENTS

{Chapter 1}

SAULTY TEARS

Sometimes life isn't what we thought it would be. Whether it is the loss of a job, an unexpected diagnosis, a defiant child, or even the constant negativity of the evening news, sometimes you just feel like burying your head in the sand.

Tucked away in the pages of the Old Testament we discover a heartbroken prophet named Samuel who had reached the end of his ropes. He can't eat. He can't sleep. His eyes are swollen. His knees are brittle. One lamp flickers in the corner of the room as he rubs his tear-soaked bearded cheeks. He still can't figure out where things went wrong and if there are any possible means of salvaging the legacy of a king he vouched for and loved like a son.

His worst nightmare had come true.

The cold slap of reality came when he heard these words that the Lord spoke to Samuel, *"How long will you mourn for Saul, seeing I have rejected him...?"* (1 Samuel 16:1a). His mind rushed to Saul from every angle, each time with the same gut-wrenching results. Instead of finding Saul, he found an empty cutout of who Saul used to be—who he should be. Saul's silhouette was charred against the backdrop of Israel's history and now, suddenly, everything was in a state of flux.

How could this be? What could I have done differently?

Why didn't Saul listen to my counsel?

Samuel must have grappled with these piercing questions. But pointing the finger at Saul and hanging all the blame on him didn't make him feel any better. He felt partly responsible for this royal train wreck. After all, he had installed him as king. He also couldn't escape the happy memories that played through his mind like a movie trailer. It seemed like only yesterday he had poured oil on the head of this young and handsome man— full of potential and promise. The image of Saul standing before Israel at this inauguration was one that he couldn't erase.

Those were better times, indeed.

The hope that once etched Samuel's heart was now a hole of hopelessness. Samuel was crying "Saulty" tears over the rejection of his beloved king—which also might have felt like a rejection of himself. We can't say for sure what his internal struggle felt like. But we can creatively assume these struggles and questions, because we know the pain of hope collapsing before our very eyes. We all experience the gap between what we expect and what we experience.

Hope often fades in the gaps between reality and our dreams, between prayers prayed and prayers answered.

HOPE GAPS

Fade to black and roll the credits because Saul's story was basically over. Sure, he was still physically alive. But that was all. His life had become an empty shell of existence—dark and soulless. Once God rejects a person or a plan, there's no going back. All options are taken off the table. No bargains. No deals. Case closed. Samuel knew this. And he also knew better than to shake his fist at God in protest because Saul had already been given plenty of chances to obey. Samuel wasn't grieving Saul because he had died, but because he was alive without purpose.

We all live in a gap. It's where our dreams die and desires dry up. It's often the source of our deepest frustration and discouragement. There is no way to humanly reconcile this space between. It's a black hole of searching for answers you may never find.

In 2009, I found myself in a hope gap—a space of dis- appointment and unmet expectations. I lost my job in the summer. And by winter, I lost my house.

Losing my job was more than inconvenient; it was deva- stating. My wife, Cherie, had also just lost her job about a month before. I still remember driving home from my last day at work (for what felt like an eternity) and thinking *Now what am I going to do?* As tears streamed down my face, my mind went blank. I couldn't think of one verse to recite. None of my sermons came to mind. Every spiritual platitude I knew seemed too silly and useless to even utter out loud. It's funny how those tidy answers and Hallmark-y clichés we say to console others in their time of discouragement…never works on ourselves.

It killed me to think of walking into my house and telling my wife that I was jobless. After her lay off, we had already begun to restructure our finances. We decided she wouldn't go back to work but would become a stay-at-home mom and focus on raising our then two-year-old son Makai. It wouldn't be easy, but we had a plan. We'd figure it out and make the adjustments necessary. A little less eating out at restaurants and a little more bag-lunches for me. I would also cut back on Starbucks and brew coffee at home in the mornings (what a sacrifice). We were ready for the challenge. But…that was all based on my income, which was about to be flipped upside down.

Once I parked in my driveway, I turned off the ignition and just sat there for a minute in deafly silence. Then I took a deep breath, got out of my car and walked in. Moments later I was hugging my wife on the couch, telling her, *"I'm so sorry babe. But somehow, God will make a way."*

Months later we lost our house, not just any house, our *first* house — the one we worked tirelessly for, the one we brought our newborn son home to. We had more than money invested. We had dreams invested. It was *ours*. But because I couldn't make the payments and fell way behind, our property foreclosed.

That year I lost more than my job and my house. For a few months, I lost hope in the gap of what I expected and what I experienced. In my moments of bare honesty, I felt cheated out of my own promises. This wasn't supposed to happen. This wasn't the fairy-tale ending we had hoped for. I sunk into a hope gap and wondered when, where, and how things would improve.

Samuel's hope gap echoed with pain. He grieved Saul as if he had died.

SAULS OF THE SOUL

Like Samuel, it's hard to give up on something that you've invested so much into. It's hard to walk away from relationships and dreams you've poured time, energy, money and heart into. When our original plan falls through, it can be difficult to see any hope, to see past the dust of failure.

We've all had *Sauls of the soul*—disappointments that fracture our faith or shatter our dreams. Like Samuel, I know I *need* to move on, but my past is magnetic; its gravitational pull is the memory of what was and what should have been. Why couldn't Samuel just instantly cut ties with Saul and embrace the next chapter of his life? Why was he lingering in a season that was over? Why did this man of God sit there and sob over one disobedient king? The answer is simple. He loved Saul. He wanted this to work out so bad it hurt. But the only problem was, God had rejected Saul. Trying to accept what God rejects is a recipe for misery.

God doesn't just see our pain; He feels it.

God became Man not only to save us, but also to experience humanity at the deepest level. When his close friend Lazarus died, Jesus grieved hard. He shut out the world around Him and sobbed like a baby. The shortest verse in the Bible echoes the loudest of Jesus' humanity.

"*Jesus wept*" (John 11:35).

Not *they*. *Jesus*.

Not *prayed, preached or praised*. *Wept*.

Heaven and earth collide with two words—*Jesus wept*.

My mind's image of Jesus weeping melts away the misconception of an aloof God who relates only to my spirituality. I serve a God who knows my weak humanity and speaks the language of tears. I am flooded with the reassurance that God not only fills me, He feels me. When I hurt, He hurts.

Samuel's discouragement may have blinded him from the fact that God grieved over Saul, too. If anybody was invested in Saul, it was God—not Samuel. The Lord said: "*I greatly regret that I have set up Saul as king, for he has turned back from following Me, and has not performed My commandments.*" (1 Samuel 15:11). The regret in this passage is not about God admitting a mistake or wishing He could take back His decision. God was truly grieved at the sad outcome of Saul's choices. The relevance of Samuel's grief and yours in these dark moments is rooted in the divine grief of God.

When the blackness of disappointment presses in and your mind is channel-surfing for a positive picture, be assured that hope is not lost. When hope plays hide n' seek with your soul, keep seeking. Struggle forward, not backwards. Let your tears irrigate the garden of tomorrow's promise. Like Jesus, weep but don't let your tears blur your vision. Be angry but don't throw a fit and lose your temper. Vent but don't complain about problems you can change. Don't make long-term decisions based on short-term emotions. If so, short-term decisions will be plagued by long-term emotions.

Sauls of the soul are a part of life. God knows this. He allows this. That's why He gave Samuel time to grieve and process his disappointment. God was more concerned with the *extent* of Samuel's grief. We can't allow our history to delay our destiny.

{Chapter 2}

Seasons and Reasons

During the time when my world was sinking with foreclosure letters and food stamps, I began to wonder if God had forgotten about me. As my dollars were being stretched, so was my faith. Allow me to rewind my story a little further. Before all this happened, I had previously left a good job, stable income, family, friends and business connections to move from Northern (Bay Area) to Southern California. I left everything to start a family and build a new dream. I even turned down a great career opportunity to stay in town. But none of that mattered because I was sure that this was God's will. But now God's will became *will God?*

Will God bless me?

Will God make a way?

Will God still use my life?

In my quiet spaces, these questions screamed at me. Christians aren't supposed to ask these types of questions, especially preachers. We're supposed to have super-hero faith in times of difficulties. But can I just be honest? When your back is up against the wall, your impossibilities stare at you and the devil ramps up his lies. Suddenly, your faith feels as fragile as fine China. Still, even with my fragile faith, I silently trusted in God. The Holy Spirit handled me with care. I was not alone. Also, my immediate family and parents encouraged me. Thinking back, I don't know how I would have made it without the prayers of my church and family. The Lord carried me when I couldn't carry myself.

But one phone call changed everything.

One spring afternoon in 2009, my wife and I were walking through a thrift store when my cell phone rang. I didn't recognize the number. Like a lot of people, I usually let unknown numbers go to voicemail. But for some reason I felt to answer this time. On the other line was someone I barely knew at the time—Pastor Omar Cortez, who was the Secretary for the National Messengers of Peace (MOP). I was caught a little off guard, but as he began to share the reason for his call, I became both excited and nervous at the same time. He called on behalf of the National MOP, inviting me to preach at an upcoming National Youth Advance in Phoenix, Arizona.

I had never preached or even stood on the platform for a national event. I was humbled that the national board would even consider me. It took a couple of hours to sink in. Okay, maybe a day or two.

This was God's way of asking me, *"How long will you grieve?"* I've discovered that when things are falling apart, God is building you up for something greater. Maybe you're thinking; *it was just one phone call, one invitation, one speaking engagement, it doesn't seem like that big of a deal.* It does when you're searching for any sign of hope, any clue that God still has a plan. The reason that one phone call changed my life was because it opened the doors to a ministry that I never could have imagined. One phone call shut the devil's mouth and renewed my faith in God.

Ever since that phone call, my life has never been the same. One speaking engagement led to being invited to preach before a large audience at the National Youth Convention in Anaheim. Shortly thereafter I was summoned to a Coordinator role with the MOP that allowed me to tour the country and minister to thousands of youth. Two years later, I was elected National Secretary—the same position Pastor Cortez occupied when he called me to preach that one spring afternoon in the aisle of a thrift store. As of today, I've since been elected and now serve as President of the National MOP and have been afforded the opportunity to preach before thousands and minister throughout the world.

Please hear me: I take no credit, nor do I boast. All honor and glory belong to Jesus Christ! I'm here by His grace, because Christ within me is the hope of glory. Looking back, I wonder what would have happened if I had allowed my disappointments to pollute my attitude and become bitter towards God or other people. But I believe God was preparing me for that unknown call. When I realized that God was asking me *"How long will you mourn?"* I knew I had to let go of my plans and allow His grace to carry me into the next season. In order to embrace *what is*, you must let go of *what was*.

That was then; this is now.

STUCK IN THE UNSEASONS

The Bible teaches, *"To everything there is a season. A time for every purpose under heaven…A time to weep, And a time to laugh; A time to mourn, And a time to dance"* (Eccl. 3:1, 4). Samuel had his moment to grieve and be upset. But at some point, God must have thought *enough is enough.* Therefore, God interrupted Samuel's pity-party with a question He could also be asking you today: *"How long will you mourn over what didn't work out?"* God didn't violate life's seasons; He honored them…to the point of alerting the prophet of when it was time to move on.

Samuel was stuck in the season of Saul, an era that God dismissed, a time period I would refer to as "un-seasons."

In most professional team sports, they have something called the "off-season," which is an extended period of rest and preparation between seasons of official play. In a spiritual sense, we do experience off-seasons—times of refreshment, introspection, and preparation for what's next. Samuel wasn't in the off-season. He was in the un-season—an overdue timeframe that delayed God's official plan. I wonder how often we delay the power of hope because we're stuck in the un-seasons of life?

Hope diminishes in the un-season.

Here's a question: why do we insist on staying in seasons that are over? Here's another one: why don't we usually recognize what God rejects? We have an innate propensity to reject what God accepts. And on the flip side, we tend to accept or desire what God rejects. There is probably a myriad of reasons why we stay stuck in expired seasons of life, instead of moving on. There are three distinct reasons for un-seasons, which I'll explore in the pages to follow.

CROWD CONTROL

The first reason for un-seasons is *people,* both living and deceased, whom we allow to control our decisions. Although Samuel knew he would never see Saul again, he couldn't embrace the idea of meeting someone new, someone different. The memory of Saul still haunted him. Maybe he felt partly responsible for the way things turned out. After all, it was Samuel who proclaimed and inaugurated Saul as king over Israel. He struggled to let go of Saul because they shared time together. Perhaps he felt guilty about moving forward because it would mean leaving Saul behind to fend for himself.

Samuel couldn't anoint the next king of Israel, David, until he parted ways with Saul. He had to accept the reality that things were over and would never be the same again. If you've ever had to let go of a relationship, the hardest truth to swallow could be that you'll never be able to recreate what you had with him or her. Forcing yourself to feel something that isn't there is a waste of energy and possibly detrimental to your wellbeing. Samuel and Saul didn't just naturally grow apart like some friendships do—*God rejected Saul.*

You can't bring everybody from your past into your future. Not everyone you're connected to right now is capable of accompanying you on your journey. The Bible says in Amos 3:3, *"Can two walk together, unless they are agreed?"* Don't let the wrong relationships deprive you of your divine purpose. Who's holding *you* back? Maybe it's time to let them go. Don't let people from your past define your potential by reminding you of your old self, old belief systems or old habits. As Samuel would later realize, a new relationship can unleash a fresh anointing.

The older I get, the more I realize this principle. As a young teen and twenty-something, I lived with the naïve notion that my friends would be my *friends till the end.* But I learned that some friends will naturally drift away and others must be intentionally let go. Some friends were there for me during a season. But once that season was over, their significance in my life vanished. I even tried to hang on to a few whom I genuinely thought were "my friends," only to realize that their toxic opinions or lifestyles were not helping me progress as an individual.

I'm reminded of the beautiful character of Ruth—who left Moab to follow her mother-in-law Naomi back to Bethlehem. Ruth famously pledged to Naomi: *"Your people shall be my people"* (Ruth 1:16). She realized that in order to embrace the hope of a better future, her relationships had to change. Ruth had to be open to meeting and befriending new people from a difficult culture. Her past friends and associates—including her sister-in-law, Orpah—couldn't handle the journey.

Are there certain people in your life that you need to break away from? Has God rejected a relationship that you're struggling to end? Letting people go is not about stepping on them to get ahead or puffing yourself up; it's about getting past your un-season. There is no virtue in clinging to relationships that undermine your spiritual development. Create a safe distance from those who push your buttons and are determined to misunderstand you.

THERE'S NO PLACE LIKE HOME

In the 1939 classic film *The Wizard of Oz*, Dorothy famously tapped her sparkly red heels together three times and repeated, "There's no place like home." Suddenly she regained consciousness on her bed, surrounded by her family and dog, Toto. Indeed, there's no place like home. But I would like to modify this legendary line to say, "There's no place like...*being where God wants you*." I know it doesn't have the same ring to it. But it's true nonetheless.

The second reason we stay stuck in the un-seasons are *places*. The Lord told Samuel, "...*Fill your horn with oil, and go; I am sending you to Jesse the Bethlehemite. For I have provided Myself a king among his sons*" (1 Samuel 16:1). Samuel couldn't fulfill his purpose by staying where he was. The next king, David, wasn't just going to land on his doorstep. He had to pack up and go.

After losing my house, I realized that I couldn't stay in

Southern California—not because I didn't want to, but because my season had expired. The brook had dried up and I found myself panting after God and His will for my life. Gentle but clear whispers began to echo in my spirit, *it's time to move back to the Bay Area.* I'll be honest. That's not what I wanted to hear. Return home with my tail between my legs, feeling like a failure?

No thank you.

Then I rationalized. *"Lord, I'd rather grind it out here and recreate the life we wanted. Why can't you just bless me here? Didn't you call me here in the first place?"* But at this point, I was simply dancing around what I knew was inevitable.

So, one Saturday morning at 6:00 AM, with our moving truck loaded and coffee cups filled, we embarked on a 400-mile trek to San Jose. As we drove, the warm sun felt like heaven's floor-heater thawing out the fears that nearly froze my faith from moving on. When we arrived at our destination, I knew it was the start of a new season. I was at peace. And I've learned that peace in uncertain times is better than fear in certain times. Sounds backwards, right? But it's true.

The following principle has shaped many of my decisions over the years: "The right thing at the wrong *time*, is the wrong thing." However, I've recently discovered a similar yet equally important principle: "The right thing in the wrong *place*, is the wrong thing." Nature illustrates this perfectly. If you plant a green fern in the desert, it will die. If you plant a cactus in the desert, it will thrive. Where you're planted could either stimulate or limit your growth.

God is a God of places. The creation narrative tells the story of a God who planted a garden and placed man inside of it. This was a location specifically designed for Adam to function and enjoy fellowship with God. Likewise, Abram had to leave his country and family in order to occupy his Promised Land.

In the New Testament, places still have meaning and significance. God allowed the apostle Paul to visit some places and not others. Paul was *"forbidden by the Holy Spirit to preach the word in Asia"* (Acts 16:6). Asia in this context isn't a reference to the largest continent. The term *Asia* in the first century represented what is now the modern-day country of Turkey. My point is simply that places are connected to spiritual seasons. Staying in a place, a company, a church, a city, a school, or a certain cultural environment could be the reason for your un-season. Is it possible that you are looking for the right thing in the wrong place?

Ruth pledged to Naomi *"...wherever you lodge, I will lodge"* (Ruth 1:16). This wasn't easy for this young widow, because leaving Moab meant leaving the place where she and her husband had built a life and dreamed of starting a family. Leaving home felt like she was betraying his memory. But surrounded by painful reminders—the smell of his shirts, and the silent echoes of his voice down the hall—she realized that she couldn't stay in that place anymore. At some point she stopped mourning, and starting hoping again. Naomi was her ticket out of her un-season.

Ruth understood that her destiny had a *destination*. She couldn't lodge in Moab and expect the promises of Bethlehem. She had to move on. It was more than a change of scenery, but a repositioning of purpose. You can't expect new promises when you're lodged in old places. A tree's fruit depends on the soil it's planted in. Your greatest level of fruitfulness is first determined by where you're planted. Maybe you're frustrated because you've been watering and watering and watering your dream, yet no fruit has produced. No amount of water will change the soil you're planted in. Therefore, make sure you're planted in the right place to fulfill God's calling for your life—to break out of your un-season.

LOOKS ARE DECEIVING

The third reason for staying stuck in the un-season is *perception*. In order for Samuel to embrace hope and recognize his next season, he needed to change the lenses he was looking through. His idea of a king looked dramatically different than God's idea. Samuel's initial confidence in Saul was based almost entirely on his physical stature and striking appearance. He *looked* like a king. Even though God chose Saul to be Israel's first king, Samuel was sold once he laid eyes on him. Samuel was impressed by what he saw on the outside. So were the Israelites. They were enraptured with the image that Saul portrayed. But looks are deceiving. In the end, it was the unseen character flaws that brought him down.

When Samuel arrived at Jesse's house, his perception hadn't fully changed. He was still looking through the old lenses. Before the formal interviews began, His eyes darted to the young man who fit the image of a king. But it was a misfire: *"So it was, when they came, that he looked at Eliab and said,*

"Surely the LORD's anointed is before Him!" (1 Samuel 16:6). False perceptions lead to false predictions. When you "think" you know what's best based on your own limited understanding or feelings, you can completely miss the will of God. You may end up making predictions about your life, about people, or situations that conflict with God's agenda. The tragedy occurs when we attempt to appoint what God hasn't appointed.

Many disappointments began as *misappointments*. Microsoft Word just underlined the word "misappointment" in red zigzags because it's not in the dictionary. But luckily it's in *my* dictionary. I would define *misappointments* as simply missed appointments or missing the point. We miss the point when we look for benchmarks that God doesn't and even advises us against. Samuel almost recreated the same problem by picking Eliab—a young man who looked every bit the part. It's a good thing Samuel didn't voice his selection too loudly. Or else it would have created a very awkward scenario for him. That's not something a prophet wants on his resume—a "You're it! Oops, just kidding" incident.

God interrupted Samuel's thought process and said: *"Do not look at his appearance or at his physical stature, because I have refused him. For the Lord does not see as man sees; for man looks at the outward appearance, but the Lord looks at the heart"* (1 Samuel 16:7).

Light bulb.

Now it makes sense.

This was Samuel's "aha moment." I really wish there were an extra verse between verses 7 and 8 to know what he felt. Samuel kept it cool and orderly, as he nodded "no" to Eliab. This wasn't just a fine-tuning of his vision, but a 180-degree shift in perception. Maybe there was a frightened tingling sensation in his fingers and toes as he thought about how close he came to choosing the wrong man. He needed to change the way he viewed his situation and opportunity. People stay stuck in the un-seasons because they still have the wrong perception.

You will never grow beyond your perception. If you see yourself as a victim or damaged goods, your negative view will influence negative choices. It's time to change your perception about yourself and realize that you deserve better because you're God's child. If you can perceive your blessings, you can receive your blessings.

Do you need healing? See yourself healed.

Do you need a relationship restored? See it happening.

Do you have a dream? See it fulfilled.

Don't be deceived by the appearance of your present circumstances. The Lord told Abram *"Lift your eyes now and look from the place where you are—northward, southward, eastward, and westward; for all the land which you see I give to you and your descendants forever"* (Genesis 13:14). Lift your eyes and gain a blessed perception of your life. Gaze upon the prospect of greener pastures. Like Abram, you cannot wait until you've arrived before you visualize your promises. You must perceive it before you receive it. "Look from the place where you are." Hope sees ahead. It doesn't deny reality, but denies the finality of reality.

Like the prodigal son's father, hope wakes up every morning and stands on a gloomy hillside for the slight chance that a repented son will emerge in the distance. Get your eyes off the past and what could have been. There is hope if you're willing to look beyond the obvious, beyond the outward evidence, and discover God's hidden treasures.

You've heard the expression, "Don't judge a book by its cover." Samuel almost made that mistake. If he had, I wonder if a young harp-playing shepherd named David would have missed his moment to become king. The content, not the cover, tells the real story. Your story isn't over yet. The *Author and Finisher* of your faith is about to dip His pen and write the next chapter of your life.

{Chapter 3}

The Grace Prism

On December 4, 2012, my iPhone buzzed on my desk at work. That small vibration would rock my entire world. The moment I answered the phone, I heard my wife Cherie's tearful voice, "Jacob, something's happened." I swallowed a gulp of air as a million thoughts raced across my brain. Since she was seven months pregnant, I immediately thought of our baby.

"What's wrong? Are you okay?" I asked, afraid to hear the answer.

"Yes, I'm okay. But I just got home and found our house broken into. The police just got here."

"I'm on my way." Then I raced home.

When I pulled up to our house and saw the police cars parked outside I realized that this wasn't just a minor mash-and-grab. I jumped out of my car and rushed to my wife who was crying in the driveway, holding my son Makai's hand. With my arms wrapped around her, I whispered, "It's okay, babe, I'm here."

When I stepped through the front door of my house, it looked like a war zone. Our house was totally ransacked. Our things were thrown everywhere. Drawers were pulled out and emptied. Expensive electronics and laptops were gone. Watches and trinkets were cleaned out.

Stepping over mounds of clothes I slowly walked towards the kitchen and saw our back door completely smashed open. Then I saw the shoeprint of the boot that kicked the door from the outside. Honestly, that shoeprint bothered me more than anything else. It angered me that someone violated my home and violently kicked my door so hard that the doorframe holding the deadbolt splintered off the wall. I couldn't erase that image from my mind. It wasn't so much *what* the burglars stole, but *how* they stole it. I've been robbed before, but this felt different. It wasn't just another random home robbery. My spirit felt attacked.

I know a home robbery isn't the worst thing that can happen in life. On a scale of tragic events and human pain, it ranks nowhere near the sudden loss of life, human suffering, or injustice. I can't compare a home intrusion to the atrocities or evil that flashes across the evening news. But personal times of crisis can pull the floor out from beneath you and make you aware of just how unpredictable life is.

The word *crisis* originates from the Greek word *krisis,* meaning "to sift or separate." We have all been *or* will be sifted in some way. I'm sorry. I know that's not what you want to hear. I didn't enjoy typing it. I wish I could delete that sentence from this paragraph. But I can't, because it's the brutal reality of life. We simply cannot control the outcome of every situation. Life is messy and fragile. People can be unpredictable and fickle. Health isn't 100% guaranteed no matter what choices you make. We humans attempt to control the rhythm of life and etch our plans in stone. At best, we can limit our risks, but will never eliminate them.

I repeat. A home robbery isn't the worst thing can that happen in life. But sometimes one life event can trigger a series of events, a chain reaction of hurt and disappointment. Before I could pick up the broken pieces of the robbery, crisis would kick down another door. This time the shoeprint wasn't on my house, but on my heart.

THIS CAN'T BE HAPPENING

Shaken up from the break in, we decided to stay at my parents' house until we could sort things out. Besides, there was no way we could sleep comfortably at home. It was the second night at my parents, after my son had just gone to bed, when my wife walked over to me and said, "I don't feel good." I quickly noticed her hands gently rubbing her tummy. Then with a look of uncertainty, she whispered, "I think it's the baby. I'm not sure."

"What do you feel?" I asked.

"I can't explain it. But something isn't right."

Five minutes later we were driving to the hospital, just to be safe. It didn't seem too serious at the time, but we didn't want to take any chances either. I thought: *Just a little checkup and maybe some pills and we'd be on our way home. Shouldn't be too bad,* It turns out I was wrong. Way wrong.

After being checked by a few nurses and a doctor, we started to think maybe we could leave soon. As we sat there in a dimly lit ER room, a nurse walked in to get something, so my wife asked, "When will I be able to go home?"

The nurse smiled and said, "Honey, you ain't going nowhere until this baby is born."

Immediately my wife and I looked at each other like *"this can't be happening."*

Then the nurse added, "The baby can come at any time. Tomorrow. Next week. Next month. Until then, you're officially on bed rest."

Since my wife's water bag was slowly leaking, it was a race against time as to when our baby girl would be born. But in that moment, at around 3:00 AM, we learned two things. First, she couldn't leave the hospital. Second, our baby girl would be born very premature—and her life was uncertain.

Two very long weeks later, our princess Chloe came into the world—all 3.9 lbs. of her. But the celebration soon collided with the realities of her premature birth. For days we couldn't hold her, but could only reach into the armholes of the incubator and caress her tiny hands. My soul was shredded as I watched my baby cling to life, hooked up to so many machines and wires.

Not being able to take her home was painful, especially for my wife whose maternal instincts were gasping for air.

Over the course of a month we drove to and from the hospital every day. Little by little we witnessed a painful expression of God's grace. We celebrated her survival one "removed" wire at a time. Many times I drove home from the hospital with tears streaming down my face, trying to figure out why my world had caved in. In those moments where my life throbbed with uncertainty, grace became the anthem of my soul.

Peering into the plastic box where my baby spent her days and nights, I was engulfed in the tides of grace. Before this series of events, between police stations and hospitals, I thought of grace as just a pardon of sin. But my trials taught me that grace is much more than sin management or undeserved favor. God's prism *is* grace, which refracts the colorful character of God into life's many dimensions and experiences. Those moments of grace anchored my belief that God would not only amuse us, but amaze us.

I'd like to suggest three expressions of God's grace in the midst of disappointment.

FROM HOPEFULLY TO FULL OF HOPE

The first expression of God's prism of grace is *hope*. This entire book is about hope. But hope is rooted in the grace of God. Quite simply, if God were not gracious, we would have no hope. Let's consider what the Word of God says: *"Now may our Lord Jesus*

Christ Himself, and our God and Father, who has loved us and given us everlasting consolation and good hope by grace, comfort your hearts and establish you in every good word and work" (2 Thessalonians 2:16-17). The phrase in focus is "good hope by grace." That needs to sink into our minds. The NIV translation says, *"by his grace gave us...good hope."* The NCV translation says, *"through his grace he gave us a good hope."* Hope flows through the prism of grace and thrusts its rays into the darkness of disappointment.

Grace turns "hopefully" into "full of hope." We don't just cross our fingers and wish upon a star. Through God's grace, we hope with a daring confidence, a brave assurance that God will ultimately make a way. Maybe feeling hopeless is the result of feeling graceless. Maybe we lose hope because we lose sight of God's sovereign grace—the beauty of His consolation and love. If hope is based squarely on grace, then grace must be present in all my circumstances. Grace doesn't usually announce itself in our grief. We simply feel something in the chamber of our souls, an undercurrent of peace that calms the hailstorm.

God's grace instills hope that comforts and restores steadiness in our lives. Worldly hope provides only temporal doses of happiness that rise and fall based on our circumstances. But our heavenly hope is anchored to a Rock—Jesus Christ—who is the same yesterday, today and forever. We are comforted to know that God surrounds the trouble that surrounds us.

There is no greater hope in the universe than in the One who freckled the cosmos with stars and lit the sun on fire with nothing but His spoken Word. One word of hope can rescind our darkness and ignite forgotten dreams. Even fragile hope dispels our fears and frustrates our frustrations.

God double dares us to hope.

WEAK DAYS

The second expression of grace for us to consider is *strength*. No matter how bad you want to believe, it's hard to trust God when you've been through a minefield and had pieces of you blown away. Even when you attempt to move on, some hurts and memories stay lodged in your heart like shrapnel. There are some pieces from your past that you can't leave behind, because they're embedded in you and ultimately shape the person you've become—for better or worse. Some of our personal struggles are deeply wedged in our lives like permanent splinters, no matter how desperately we pray for their removal.

The Apostle Paul, the writer of over half the New Testament, battled secret afflictions that couldn't be simply prayed away. Paul said in 2 Corinthians 12:7-8, "…*Therefore, in order to keep me from becoming conceited, I was given a thorn in my flesh, a messenger of Satan, to torment me. Three times I pleaded with the Lord to take it away from me.*" Paul labeled his private struggle "a thorn in my flesh." This imagery isn't pleasant no matter what angle or spiritual lenses you look through. You can't dress up a thorn with fancy words or religious phrases so it sounds like an enjoyable experience. A thorn is an undeniable source of pain or contention.

Frustration boils in the pot of unanswered prayers—when we feel like God isn't hearing us, or worse—He hears but doesn't respond. We pound the floor and empty our boxes of Kleenex. Still, the answer clashing against our will is "no." Our hearts wrestle with questions. *No? That's your final answer? Is this a test of my determination? Lord, are you just prolonging my solution, my healing, my miracle until I'm more prepared? Are you going to change your mind?*

Paul realized that God did, in fact, answer him. The issue is he didn't like the answer he got. After three desperate attempts to change God's mind and remove the struggle, Paul gained an unexpected revelation of God's grace. He discovered that God's "no" serves His purpose in the same way as His "yes." We assume that only "yes" advances the plan of God in our lives. However, a divine "no" has the same power as a "yes." It just doesn't feel good or agrees with our sensibilities.

Life has thorns, unwelcomed struggles that annoy you like a crooked picture-frame hung high above your reach. Life would be better and sweeter if you could tilt that one pesky dysfunction back into place. But it rarely occurs to us that the frame was left crooked on purpose, that the struggle, the weakness or imperfection reveals the character of God and ultimately serves His purpose. Instead of trying to adjust every slanted frame in your life, adjust your perception. When you can't tilt your problems, tilt your head. Change your thinking and see things from God's point of view. He allowed weakness to shape your perspective on grace, love and compassion—to humanize you in ways that permit the gospel to shine in you and through you.

Paul states his understanding of God's no: *"in order to keep me from becoming conceited."* God wouldn't remove the thorn because it served a purpose, it kept Paul's ego in check. Without question, the sharp edge of the thorn stabs our pride; it bursts the bubble of our egos and exaggerations. But humility is merely a secondary benefit—a byproduct of the struggle. The greater purpose of thorns is not merely to prevent pride in our hearts, but to reveal the grace of God.

In the following passage, the apostle explains the main purpose of his thorn: *"9 But he said to me, "My grace is sufficient for you, for my power is made perfect in weakness." Therefore I will boast all the more gladly about my weaknesses, so that Christ's power may rest on me. 10 That is why, for Christ's sake, I delight in weaknesses, in insults, in hardships, in persecutions, in difficulties. For when I am weak, then I am strong"* (2 Corinthians 12:9-10). Through the prism of grace, God's strength shines in our weakness. He sustains us through life's most disappointing times. What I discovered as I held my daughter no further than the wires would reach, was that grace was holding me.

Like Paul, I heard the whisper of my Creator say, *"My grace is sufficient for you."* This type of grace meets us at our point of need and strengthens us with courage and wisdom. Above all, grace awakens my soul to the presence of God. I'm reminded that He will never leave me nor forsake me. Mercy blushes at the sight of grace. When I sit in the messes of my own making, I plead for mercy, but God goes beyond and stretches His grace around me like a rubber band.

My thorns of weakness qualify me for greater measures of God's sustaining power. How else can you experience or appreciate God's strength, unless you confess your area of weakness? I would have never known God as a healer, unless I was sick, unless my daughter had been hooked up to machines. I would have never truly have known Him as my provider until my streams of income dried up. It's usually when I feel the least qualified to preach or pastor, that God uses me the greatest. Don't get me wrong. I'm not "trying" to be weak. But I've stopped pretending to be strong in areas that I'm not. Faking your strengths only magnifies your weaknesses. But confessing your weaknesses magnifies God's strength. Paul said, "*I will boast all the more gladly about my weaknesses, so that Christ's power may rest on me.*" Allow me to put it this way: Your greatest limitation is God's greatest platform.

Paul punctuated his thoughts with this confession, "*For when I am weak, then I am strong.*" This opposes our natural line of thinking, which says that our strengths make us strong. We're supposed to *lean on our strengths*. I certainly agree with the idea of leveraging our strengths and skills to earn a better living and add the most value to others. God gave you natural-born abilities and strengths. But we all wrestle with weaknesses (thorns) in one form or another.

Maybe your teenager is rebelling or shutting you out.

Maybe your bills keep piling up.

Maybe you feel like your marriage is on life-support.

Maybe you're fighting cancer and don't feel like fighting anymore or being a burden on your loved ones.

Maybe you feel unqualified about your calling.

God's perfect strength will manifest through our imperfections. Whatever need or weakness you're struggling with, it's an opportunity for the grace of God to support you beyond your own ability. In fact, Jesus wants to shine through your life in unexplainable ways—defying logic and the laws of nature. The more impossible the situation, the more glory God receives.

God can turn shattered glass into stained glass, mistakes into miracles, hurts into halos. He is using your weakness to draw you closer to Him and to His purpose for your life.

King David made a perplexing observation when he said, *"I am weak today, though anointed king"* (2 Samuel 3:39). Seems like a contradiction doesn't it? Wouldn't an anointing of the Holy Spirit prevent a mental and physical depletion? How is it possible to be both weak and anointed at the same time? Doesn't God's favor cancel our frustrations?

Well, actually no it doesn't. The Christian life can be a puzzling oxymoron—like being spiritually willing but physically weak, or being joyful amid suffering. These divine dichotomies are seedbeds for the grace of God to flourish and humility to sprout. Plainly speaking, it's exactly where God wants you. You could often describe life in David's terms. Weak, though anointed. Hurt, though loved. Struggling, though content. Broken, though blessed. That's precisely where you learn to depend on God and find purpose in your pain. This concept shows up again and again in this book because it's directly related to the issue of hopelessness.

GRACE PERIODS

Most banks and creditors give their customers a *grace period*. Wikipedia defines "grace period" *as a time past the deadline for an obligation during which a late fee that would have been imposed is waived.*[1] Grace periods are meant to reduce the stress of paying your bill on the due date, in case you cannot for some unforeseen reason. I would like to borrow this term and use it for a different purpose, specifically to introduce the third expression of grace in God's prism—*time*.

We want timely miracles. But God also gives the miracle of time. We want blessings *now*, but sometimes the blessing *is* now. If you can embrace that truth (no matter how hard), it could dramatically change how you interpret God's purpose in your life. In some cases, time is the miracle.

I'm reminded of when Joshua earnestly prayed for the sun to stand still, granting the Israelites time to utterly defeat their enemies in battle. In some cases, *time* is the miracle. Through time, our souls awaken to God's sovereign grace and glory. Time teaches us to treasure moments, both in solitude and togetherness. It empowers us to appreciate what we have and even why we have it.

But time isn't always pleasant. It can be brutal. Proverbs 13:12 says, *"Hope deferred makes the heart sick, But when the desire comes, it is a tree of life."* Amen to that. When things don't fall into place according to our timeline, our hearts sicken with worry or depression. There's nothing pleasant about watching cancer squeeze the life out of your spouse in slow motion. There's nothing enjoyable about seeing your dreams of a successful business sink into bankruptcy. Waiting for your son or daughter to come back to God can feel like an eternity. Your injury could be taking longer than expected to heal and you feel like life is passing you by. Maybe you're shaking your head *no* and thinking…*If this is grace, I don't want it!*

I felt that way, too. But as people prayed for my family, God's grace began to surround us in greater measure. Your journey as a Christ-follower will lead you from *saving* grace to *sustaining* grace. The grace that saved you from sin and separation from God is the same grace that will preserve you through life's struggles and disappointments.

As we sat there in ICU, days became weeks, and weeks became months. All I wanted to do was bundle up my baby girl and bring her home. My wife just wanted to hold her in the same rocking chair she did with our son Makai when he was a baby. We wanted things to be *normal* again. But it was in those painful moments of waiting that grace swept low and enabled me to see beauty. Behind the feeding tubes and heart monitors, was a living, breathing, tiny human being who got stronger with each passing day. I realized that I could use my time to either complain about my problems and woes, or I could worship God and thank Him for the gift of life. Grace surprised me with the strength to savor the moment.

Even though this rough side of grace isn't attractive to us, it reveals a benevolent God who not only *heals* our pain, but *feels* our pain. I love what the writer says in Hebrews 4:15-16, *"For we do not have a High Priest who cannot sympathize with our weaknesses, but was in all points tempted as we are, yet without sin. Let us therefore come boldly to the throne of grace, that we may obtain mercy and find grace to help in time of need."*

Jesus Christ relates to our pain and disappointments on the most basic human level. He literally knows what you're going through and how you feel. On that premise, the Word of God dares us to boldly approach His throne in prayer with our deepest needs and deficiencies. I can't overlook the fact that God's throne is the "throne of *grace.*" A king's throne represents

His dominion and authority. It is also a place of royal judgment and decision-making. But as a born-again believer, you have unrestrained access to God's throne room.

Walk-ins are welcomed. No appointment necessary.

The blood of Jesus Christ covers our sins with His righteousness and ushers us into the holy of holies—the presence of God. When there, we are prone to cry out for mercy, but God grants us grace. Jesus' death and resurrection make it possible for us to obtain mercy and grace—no matter what your situation looks like.

Don't sit alone in your pain.

Don't cry outside heaven's door like a stray cat.

You are God's beloved child. Step into the *grace place*. God wants to turn your bitter water into sweet springs—disgrace into grace. He'll give you beauty for ashes, joy for mourning, and a garment of praise for the spirit of heaviness. Grace is released in your *time* of need as the Holy Spirit sustains you. Unfortunately, you cannot rush God's timing. He doesn't always operate on the timetable we want Him to. Sometimes it feels like God is oblivious to your needs or simply forgot about you—like maybe your case file slipped through the cracks somewhere in heaven.

I can assure you that God has not forgotten about you. Even now, He is holding you up with His unseen hands. Keep turning the pages of this book and you'll see how His grace unfolds.

{Chapter 4}

Divine Delays

———————◆•◆•◆———————

What do we do when God doesn't answer the way we hoped He would? What should we feel when our heart's desire is suddenly snatched away? How do we reconcile the love of God with those painful postponements in life? These questions might frustrate us, because there are no easy answers. Yet that is the tension we often feel when our hopes are dashed, when God's timing doesn't make sense. Proverbs 13:12 says, *"Hope deferred makes the heart sick, but when the desire comes, it is a tree of life."* This little verse is squeezed in the middle of a lengthy list of adages on topics ranging from laziness, get-rich-quick schemes, and child discipline—to name a few. It's almost like King Solomon got inspired while sitting in a restaurant and quickly jotted down his thoughts on a napkin. I know that feeling. You just want to freeze time for moment so you don't forget your thought. But nevertheless, verse 12 contains a wealth of wisdom. Particularly about the cycles of hope and the pain we experience when we're forced to deal with delays.

There are a few ways to understand the term "hope deferred." Allow me to frame it this way: *hope deferred is the repeated delay of your expectations.* I believe King Solomon was referring to those times in life when what we desire most keeps moving out of reach, when our hopes are repeatedly postponed. In other words, every time you get close, the finish line moves back. A series of disappointments can cause our hopes to wane and our hearts to bleed.

Why is this? Why can't we, like machines, just shut off the desire and let go? Well, obviously, we're not machines, we're humans. And once we get hopeful about something, we strongly attach ourselves to the prospects of it being fulfilled. Hope paints a portrait of our future with the brushes of emotion and faith. The more we hope, and the more our hope absorbs our life, the more invested in that portrait we become. So, every time the portrait fades with delay or the easel collapses with disappointment, panic shadows over us.

We want God to show up on our timetable. When things are crumbling around us, we need Him *now.* Not tomorrow. Not next week. Now.

Ever felt that way? Like you couldn't wait any longer? Like every minute felt like an hour, and every hour like a day? When you need to God step on the scene, it's because the situation has already reached the boiling point, and human efforts have failed. Why is it then, when we need God to expedite our miracle, He seems to drag His feet? But I've come to realize something about how God answers prayers. When God answers no, it doesn't always mean no. Sometimes His no is really a *not yet.* When God is silent, sometimes, it's for good reason. We think that God's silence is the end of the story, but it's just a pause, a set-up for a climax. It's never over until God says it's over.

PAUSE FOR EFFECT

Have you ever heard the phrase "pause for effect"? *Pause for effect* describes that silent or still moment before the crescendo of a song, the climax of a dramatic acting scene, or the conclusion of a powerful statement. That orchestrated pause allows the anticipation to build. It also gives time for the viewer or listener to reflect before the next thing happens. What you think and feel during that pause, prepares you for the big moment or idea to follow. Delayed answers and ill-timed problems are the *pause for effect* moments before God performs. During these silent spaces of time, we can either draw closer to God or drift farther apart—either trust Him more. or devise our own means.

Right at this very moment, God could be using your period of silent frustration to stage your greatest comeback. You might be living in the *pause* . . . before a divine *effect.* Your most rewarding season of life may be closer than you think. That's why you can't give up now, no matter how tempting it looks. God is setting you up for something that will make the pause worth it, something that will take you from frustration to fruition.

One of the greatest instances of God's silent delay in the Bible is found in John chapter 11. To put the story in a nutshell: Lazarus is dead. Jesus is late. Martha is upset. Mary is depressed.

Martha and Mary's brother Lazarus had succumbed to his sickness. And the question on everybody's mind was "what if"? *What if Jesus had been here four days earlier? What if He had come immediately after we called Him? Maybe none of this would have happened.*

HE LOVES ME; HE LOVES ME NOT...
HE LOVES ME

Many Christians live with a wobbly view of God's love, one that vacillates between two extremes like the childhood game with flower petals: "She loves me, she loves me not." People have the tendency to base their relationship with God on their situations—falling in and out of love with God depending on how things are going. Maybe it's because people have a *puppy love* relationship with God—an intense, but relatively shallow attachment. Puppy love is based mainly on curiosity and infatuation. But that's not enough to sustain your heart through the hardships of life. Puppy love doesn't last. It's based mostly on circumstances and not truth. Love is not real until it's tested.

As Lazarus' symptoms worsened, it was clear that nothing was working and time was running out. Martha and Mary made the proverbial 9-1-1 call to Jesus who was far, but still close enough that if He hurried over to the town of Bethany, he could get to Lazarus' bedside before it was too late. Maybe Jesus was in the middle of teaching when someone leaned in and whispered in His ear: *"Lord, behold, he whom You love is sick"* (Vs. 3). They knew how deeply Jesus felt for their family and imagined that He would rush to their need. Let's consider two crucial facts in this urgent request. First, they affirmed Lazarus' special *affection*. In fact, they don't even mention his name. Instead they refer to him as "he whom You love." That's an important detail because they wanted Jesus to know, this isn't just anybody, but somebody very important to you—this is your beloved friend. Jesus loved everyone equally, but not everyone was equally close to Him. Lazarus was believed to be one of Jesus' closer friends. It was more than a general acquaintance. The Bible narrator notes this "love" because it gives us insight into their special relationship, and also because it thickens the plot.

The second crucial fact in this verse is Lazarus' *affliction*. He was critically sick and barely clinging to life. We don't know what the actual sickness was, but it was severe enough that his health probably declined faster than Martha and Mary had expected. And clearly, all medical options and home remedies had been exhausted. At that point, these sisters were just trying to keep Lazarus alive until Jesus got there. Because once He would come, surely Jesus would heal him like He's healed so many others.

So, there you have it. In one short sentence, Jesus was alerted to his friend's affection and affliction. What more do you need to know?

This is the point where any real friend drops what they're

doing and rushes to the scene. All other appointments that day should be canceled. Whatever else had been planned is nowhere near as important as being by the deathbed of your close friend—especially when you have the ability to heal him. This is where Jesus could have defied the laws of physics and flew over to Bethany like Superman and saved the day. He could have stormed the front door and said, "Cancel the flower arrangements and obituary! I'm healing him today!" Except that's not what happened. Not even close. Jesus stayed put for another two days.

Say what? This makes no sense!

John 11:6 tells us, *"When He heard that he was sick, He stayed two more days in the place where He was."* Instead of running over to comfort them, Jesus waited and was silent. This was not the response Martha and Mary wanted. It's certainly not what I would have expected. But hear me clearly. God always has a good reason for why He doesn't move according to our plan, even if it screams in the face of logic. I know it's not easy hearing that. I know it seems to counteract our beliefs about God's love and grace. Yet something deep within nudges us to trust Him, even against human reason.

Martha and Mary sat there baffled and rattled to their core. Grieving their brother's untimely death and trying to wrap their heads around what happened, all they could do was hold each other and cry. There would be no healings to celebrate – no last-minute prayers to answer. I imagine that at times they felt more angry than sad. Maybe they even blamed themselves, too. *What if we had notified Jesus sooner rather than later? Maybe we could have figured out a way to transport Lazarus to wherever*

Jesus was, no matter how costly or inconvenient! Of course, I'm only speculating. But one thing is for sure, Martha, the more vocal of the two sisters, had begun to rehearse in her mind what she wanted to tell Jesus the moment they crossed paths again. It would not be pleasant. Raw feelings would be expressed. She wasn't going to let Jesus off the hook that easily. She loved the Lord with all her heart, which is why she wanted answers—which is why this tragedy hurt so badly.

Because if God loves me, how could He allow this to happen?

If God is love, why am I hurting, and why can't I hear Him? Have you ever felt that way? I have. And sometimes I don't know what hurts more, my wound, or what feels like God's lack of concern. I know He loves me, but I want to *feel* He loves me. I think that's normal. Isn't that what we all crave? Isn't that supposed to separate us from all other religious groups in the world—that our God is alive and accessible? Yet there are times in our lives that we're left trying to reconcile God's love with His silence. But I've come to an understanding that my heart cannot be trusted.

Our feelings are not the truest or most reliable indicators of God's presence. Our hearts are deceptive and limited in their ability to detect the unseen providence and presence of the Lord. Which is why we cannot rely on our feelings to inform our decisions. Which is why we cannot always believe the signals that our hearts are sending. Which is why the devil seeks to distort our view of God's love and erase God's faithfulness from our memory banks.

God's silence is not His absence.

He's closer to you than you think. He promised to never

leave you nor forsake you. He promised to fight your battles. He promised to catch your cares when you cast them heavenward. He promised to be with you to ends of the earth. No matter what you're feeling or what you've suffered through, I wrote this book to tell you to, "Hope Again!" It's not over until God says it's over. The case isn't closed until He closes it. You're closer to your miracle than your situation implies. Your problem is God's platform to reveal His power.

CONFLICTED HEARTS

Contrary to what many assume, God is not driven primarily by our need, but by our faith. The Bible teaches, *"Now faith is the substance of things hoped for and the evidence of things not yet seen"* (Hebrews 11:1). In God's economy, faith is the currency by which divine transactions occur; even when our faith is feeble and shaken, even when it's small and barely noticeable. Faith moves the heart of God.

Martha and Mary knew this, which is why they so desperately wanted Jesus to come to Bethany and see their sick brother. They believed in the God who heals.

The two sisters were still heartbroken and confused when they heard that Jesus was en route to Bethany. Finally, Jesus was coming. But what was the point? Jesus was late; *too* late. Maybe the grieving sisters sat across from each other, shaking their heads in disbelief, wondering if Lazarus would still be alive had Jesus got there sooner.

Maybe they thought: *That's nice, He finally decided to come, but it's too late. We wanted a healer, not a grief counselor. We needed a miracle, not a parable. What was so important that He couldn't get here BEFORE Lazarus died? We've seen Him heal and perform miracles for others many times. Why not now? Why not us?*

Once Martha heard that Jesus had been sighted on the outskirts of Bethany, she dropped what she was doing and hurried outside into the heat. She wasn't going to sit around and wait for Jesus to knock on her door. She was done waiting. So, putting one foot in front of the other, she marched into the horizon to catch Jesus before He arrived. As soon as Martha spotted Him, her heart sank. She was upset, but wanted to be *more* upset. With every step, she felt her knees getting brittle and her eyes welling up with tears. Then within yards of Jesus, her mind went blank as they made eye contact. She was still upset, but an overwhelming peace quieted her soul. Putting all arguments aside, she must have felt relieved just to be in His presence. Grieved, but grateful. Lonely, but loved. Confused, but comforted. For a moment, I believe Martha wasn't sure whether she wanted to adore Him or implore Him, worship or complain. What came out of her mouth next is one of the more honest and daring statements of faith recorded in the Bible.

"Lord, if You had been here, my brother would not have died. But even now I know that whatever You ask of God, God will give You" (John 11:21-22).

Martha was never afraid to speak her mind. Remember the time she complained about Mary sitting at Jesus' feet and not pulling her weight in the kitchen? But this time, she was more careful with her choice of words. Furthermore, her venting revealed a conflicted heart, or more so, a passive-aggressive faith. She said, *"Lord, if you had been here, my brother would not have died."* Her sister Mary would later repeat the exact same thing (Ref. John 11:32). It sounded like they were blaming Jesus without actually saying it.

Aren't we all a little guilty of doing this? I know I am.

On occasion, don't we all have passive-aggressive faith in God? I know I do.

We may not outright blame Jesus when awful things happen, but we're conflicted to know that He could have prevented those things. I realize this line of thought makes us uncomfortable. Wrestling with God's non-action pulls us into a mental space that we pretend doesn't exist, and then foolishly attempt to "cover for God" with religious platitudes and blanket statements. But Martha vocalized what was boggling everyone else's minds. And her reverent confession opens the door to a greater understanding about how God works through our pain. Unless we face the tension of His mystery, we'll never see the glory of His mastery. There must be room in your relationship with Jesus for the unknowns. If not, you will never experience the miraculous level of His power. But like Martha, if you can trust God with the pain you don't understand, He will show you His glory.

This is possibly why Jesus would say something that sounded so hurtful to His disciples, *"Lazarus is dead. And I am glad for your sakes that I was not there, that you may believe. Nevertheless let us go to him"* (John 11:14-15). Jesus did not say this to Martha or Mary, which would have added insult to injury. This was a conversation between Jesus and his disciples, prior to coming to Bethany. Still, the disciples were stumped. It has to rank as one of the more insensitive statements of Jesus. The disciples were too stunned to question Him, but I can bet their minds were racing with questions like: *Really, Lord? You're glad Lazarus died? Wasn't there some other way we could have learned about faith without someone having to die? Where are you going with this?*

However, this statement does reveal how God uses mystery as a platform for his Mastery. He lets certain things reach the end so He can unveil a new beginning. He lets certain relationships die so He can introduce you to new people. He allows certain sicknesses so He can demonstrate His authority over them through healing. Even if God doesn't cause your pain, He always uses your pain for a cause.

THIRD LEVEL FAITH

As the events unfold, both Martha and Mary battled their doubts and struggled to express their faith. They tried desperately to cope with their unmet expectations. That's not an easy process—when you're trying to fill the gap between what you hoped *would* happen versus what actually happened. What surfaced from their struggle are two levels of faith that commonly appear when we can't reconcile our dashed hopes. Level one can be called "past faith", and level two, "future faith." Let's explore each one, and then we'll consider a higher alternative to these two.

1. Past Faith
Past faith is faith for what *could* have happened. After letting Martha speak up first, Mary then emerged from her home

47

and mustered up the courage to confront Jesus with the same response as her opinionated sister: *"Lord, if You had been here, my brother would not have died"* (John 11:32). Mary seemed certain that Lazarus could still be alive if Jesus had been there four days earlier. Like Mary, many of us possess a faith for what could have been. I've noticed how easy it for people to live in the past and focus on things they can't change. They don't just speak in past tense; they live in past tense—forever dwelling on missed opportunities and alternate scenarios. They always talk about where they would be today had this or that been different. I can empathize with this sentiment. For a season, I wondered what my life could have been like…had I never lost my job, lost my house, and been forced to move 400 miles away—because I strongly believed in what God *could* have done.

From my experiences, I've learned that *past faith* does nothing to advance God's purpose in our lives. If my faith is only geared towards the past, I could argue it isn't faith at all— but remorse and regret. That's a dangerous outlook to live with. Past faith will paralyze your progress and lead into stretches of depression. It can also foster poisonous attitudes like jealousy, envy, and ungratefulness.

It's much easier to complain about the past, then to confront the present. But life is too short to live with regrets, to carry the baggage of yesterday. It's important for you to know that this book was bathed in prayer and born from my own pain. I have endeavored to stay sensitive to the Holy Spirit's voice and allow healing to flow through these pages. Therefore, hear me when I say, ***don't let your memory become your misery.*** The past is over. You cannot rewrite history. You cannot pretend you weren't hurt, disappointed or damaged. Also, stop blaming others for your unhappiness or miserable state of mind. Your faith in the past isn't helping you confront the issues that need your immediate attention.

There is no denying that our lives *could* look different had God intervened according to our wishes. But maybe God allowed it to happen, because in His supreme knowledge, there was a greater glory to be seen, a higher purpose to be fulfilled. No, that won't settle every question or defuse every emotion burning within your soul, but it will bring your heart into alignment with His. It will ensure that your life isn't lived in reverse. And it is God's plan to sooth your heart and provide sufficient grace.

Mary's statement was honest, but honestly mistaken. Here's why. God's window of opportunity opens when ours closes. With Him, there is always hope for tomorrow.

2. Future Faith

Jesus' conversation with Martha reveals a second level of faith I call *future faith*—a faith for what *would* happen: *"Jesus said to her, 'Your brother will rise again.' Martha said to Him, 'I know that he will rise again in the resurrection at the last day'"* (John 11:23-24). Martha was certain that Lazarus would rise again, but in a completely different context. She was focused on the future resurrection of the dead when the rapture of the church takes place. Her faith was real, but her expectations were postdated to a prophetic event that didn't serve their current situation. Martha's theology was spot on. Surely, the Lord will first resurrect the dead in Christ and we who are alive and remain

49

will be caught up together to meet the Lord in the skies. However, Jesus was not referring to that special event when He promised, *"Your brother will rise again."*

I'm about to speculate right now, but it seems to me like Martha knew what Jesus meant, but was simply afraid to believe it. It's almost like she didn't want to believe it. Maybe it was a defense mechanism to avoid being hurt again. We all do this from time to time. As a way of avoiding disappointment, we either set lower expectations or replace them with something else altogether.

We want to believe in something greater, but are afraid of getting too emotionally invested. For instance, you walk into the interview telling yourself you probably won't get hired. That way if you don't get the job, there is minimal investment, which means minimal disappointment. If you get into a relationship and you're afraid of being hurt like before, you won't let feelings deepen. In the short run, it "might" save you some hurt feelings; but in the long run you'll never be able to establish relationships of any real meaning or depth. It's safer and easier to say, "one day I'll find true love" – because it avoids the risk of loving the person right in front of you.

I can't prove for sure that Martha applied this logic to postponing the possible resurrection of Lazarus. Of course, if taken literally, she would have really thought that Jesus was prophesying about the rapture. But creative license allows me to consider the likelihood that she knew what Jesus meant, but didn't want to get her hopes up. I'll let you draw your own conclusion about that. But what is not up for debate is whether we humans, out of fear, tend to defend our supposed disappointments by postponing our faith.

When your faith is only based on the future, you will postpone your blessings by waiting for your circumstances to change. Like Martha, many people will bury their hopes in a time capsule and put their God-given dreams on hold.

Future faith produces spiritual farsightedness. My optometrist once told me that farsighted vision could see distant images clearly, but not close ones. They can visualize objects or words across the room, but struggle to see the same things right in front of them. Some Christians live that way. They can visualize their futures and always talk about *someday* and *one day*, but overlook the prospect of *today*. My advice is to stop watching life pass you by. Don't procrastinate your calling. Stop fantasizing about your future.

Jesus was trying to tell Martha, "The future is now." And there are areas of your life, where this same promise applies. But in order to realize them, you need to possess the third level of faith, which is *present faith*.

3. Present Faith

Although Martha had focused a portion of her faith on the unforeseen future, she also confessed to believing in what Jesus could do right then and there. She left the door open by saying, *"But even now I know that whatever You ask of God, God will give You"* (John 11:22). In the same breath of her *"if You had been here"* came the declaration of *"even now."* Martha couldn't hold back her faith. She knew that nothing was impossible for Jesus. She didn't know the specific details about how Jesus could raise a corpse that was already decomposing inside a tomb. She didn't know the how, but she knew the *who*. When you know the *who* (Jesus), the how doesn't matter.

The Bible tells us, *"This is the day the Lord has made; We will rejoice and be glad in it"* (Psalm 118:24). Mary looked to the past and Martha looked momentarily to the future. But faith is a gift that must be opened in the present. Jesus told Martha, *"I am the resurrection and the life"* (John 11:25). Jesus did not speak in past tense ("I was") nor did He in the future tense ("I will be"). He spoke in the present tense, "I am", letting Martha know that God operates in the now, in the present moment of our faith. Even if what we're hoping for is unseen or delayed, God is looking for "right now faith" in our hearts. He will do more with fragile faith in the present, then with strong faith in the past or future. God's Word says, *"Now faith is the substance of things hoped for, the evidence of things not seen"* (Hebrews 11:1). That's third-level faith! Even when the answer is delayed, my faith still lives in the moment.

THE STINK WON'T STOP HIM

When Jesus arrived to Lazarus' tomb, the laws of nature were in full swing. His body spent four days baking in a sealed tomb, in the hot Judean climate.

Knowing how badly his body had decayed and the accompanying stink of death, Martha appealed to logic, *"Lord, by this time there is a stench, for he has been dead four days"* (John 11:39). That's a true statement. No one would argue that. And apparently, Martha was still wrestling with her doubts and fears. She essentially said, *"Let's not go there. We all know Lazarus is dead. We're just trying to grieve and move forward. By opening his tomb, it's only going to unseal the ugliness of this situation. It's going to reopen our wounds. What's the point in digging up old issues? All that remains are a shell of who my brother once was. This problem stinks!"*

When problems stink in our lives, it's easier to leave them buried so we don't have to deal with them, so we don't have open up a can of worms.

We'd rather not deal with the stink of forgiving someone.

We'd rather not deal with the stink of digging through our past.

We'd rather not revisit the place where we gave up hope.

Notice that Jesus left the task of removing the stone to Martha and the others. Their miracle hinged on their willingness to give Jesus access to their pain. We often don't want to give Jesus full access to our innermost problems because we're afraid of what it might reveal. We're afraid of facing the stink of dead dreams and the dysfunctions we've tried to mask. But as I close this chapter, let me proclaim to you that the stink won't stop Him! God already knows how bad it smells. He knows your secret pain and how hard you've tried to cover it up with your own solutions.

But if you're willing to open your heart and unseal your private hurts, we serve a God who can change the outcome with just His spoken Word. In John 11:43, Jesus boldly and loudly commanded: *"Lazarus, come forth!"* Moments later a man came hobbling out the tomb with grave clothes wrapped around his whole body.

Lazarus was alive!

Death was defeated.

Martha and Mary's mouths dropped with joy.

The stink couldn't stop Jesus.

And right now, no matter how stinky, how messy, how complicated, how impossible your situation is, hope is not lost.

It's time to stop coping and start hoping.

Divine delays will stretch every fiber of your faith. Your hopes will be pushed to the edge, if not over the edge entirely. But God has a purpose in your pain. He is preparing your heart for an encounter with His glory. He is setting the stage for a display of wonder that will forever leave its imprint on your life.

{Chapter 5}

The Miracle of What's Left

O ne of my favorite sermons to preach is entitled "The Miracle of What's Left." I love this sermon for a lot of reasons, but mainly because it's so uplifting and encouraging. This powerful message centers on a rather bizarre scene found in Exodus chapter nine. Here's the backdrop of the chapter. The Israelites had suffered 400 years of arduous labor under Egyptian slavery. But God called and prepared a deliverer named Moses to emancipate His people. Since Pharaoh vigorously refused to set the Israelites free, God unleashed a series of terrifying and creepy plagues (10 in total), which eventually brought Egypt to its knees. No Hollywood special effects needed. God put on a spectacular display of power and control over the elements—not for theatrics, but to break the chains of bondage.

During those plagues, Moses found himself in the middle of an unusual test of faith. The sixth plague, in particular, provides for us our subject matter and reveals a divine truth about moving forward in victory. The key passage is found in Exodus 9:8-11:

"So the LORD said to Moses and Aaron, "Take for yourselves handfuls of ashes from a furnace, and let Moses scatter it toward the heavens in the sight of Pharaoh. And it will become fine dust in all the land of Egypt, and it will cause boils that break out in sores on man and beast throughout all the land of Egypt." Then they took ashes from the furnace and stood before Pharaoh, and Moses scattered them toward heaven. And they caused boils that break out in sores on man and beast. And the magicians could not stand before Moses because of the boils, for the boils were on the magicians and on all the Egyptians."

God instructed Moses to grab handfuls of ashes and throw them upward. Ashes are what you have left after something has burned in the fire. As it relates to life, after you've been through the fire of adversity, sometimes all you're left with are ashes—remnants of what used to be. Ashes can represent the life you once lived, the friends you once had, or the dreams that almost came true. Piles of ashes may surround you as painful reminders of what should have been, could have been, or would have been had things only gone according to plan. I'm not sure what was going through Moses' mind when God commanded him to lift those ashes up. If I were Moses, I might have been more reluctant. My response could go something like this:

You want me to do what? Uh, God...I know you're God and all, but this seems a little ridiculous. I'm supposed to take all these dirty and useless ashes and fling them up into the sky? Then somehow, this residue is supposed to mysteriously cause boils to break out on people's skin? How could this debris produce a miracle? I've seen you do weird stuff before, but I just don't see how anything good will come from something so ruined, so messy, so hopeless.

It's a good thing I'm not Moses.

God had an amazing plan that defied both human logic and possibility. When Moses took the handfuls of ashes and threw them heavenward, God supernaturally turned those ashes into a dust cloud over their enemies and afflicted their bodies with painful boils. Perhaps God is giving you the same message today: *take what you've got left and lift it heavenward.* Take the tattered remnants of your life, the little of what's leftover, the shred of hope, and lift it up to God in faith. I know it's risky. You may not be used to that type of vulnerability. But honestly, if nothing else has seemed to work and your options are slim to none, what have you got to lose? Fortunately for us, God specializes in multiplying shrinking resources and stretching our leftovers beyond imagination.

Remember the young boy with the small lunch – two fishes and five loaves? Jesus turned his snacks into a massive buffet line. There's a tendency to view the boy in this story like just a cute Sunday School character who shared his cute little meal. But what if it was his *last* meal? What if his parents or siblings were starving and waiting for him to return with groceries?

What if these fishes and loaves were all he could scrap together, all he could afford? We can only speculate the severity of his hunger and what those leftover snacks meant to him. But his faith was greater than his fears. Until we realize God's interest in what's left, what's broken, what's depleted or what's forsaken, we'll never see His creative power. God does more than tolerate our deficiencies; He uses them. He does more than accept our weaknesses; He shines His strength through them.

Joy isn't found in what you've accumulated, but in what you've surrendered in faith. Of course, it's much easier said than done. In the young boy's case, his survival was at stake. He had no tangible evidence that his risk would pay off. Those fish n' chips were more than a meal; they were the means to a miracle. God doesn't need our stuff. He wants our faith.

On the surface, Moses' ashes weren't the same as the fishes and loaves, but they both represent what's leftover or diminished. In each case, God proved that miracles come in packages we don't always recognize. Let's consider some powerful lessons that could change your life.

LET GO OF WHAT'S LOST

Many of us are fixated on what we've lost—things we'll either never get back or things that have permanently changed. We struggle to walk away from anything or anyone that we've invested our time, money, or hearts into. Have you ever struggled to accept the fact that a relationship was over or would never be the same again? Have you ever tried to reestablish a friendship with someone who has clearly changed and no longer shares the same interests as you? Do you know the feeling of fighting for job security in a fading industry? Are you still wrestling with regrets and allowing past mistakes to hold you hostage? Still licking old wounds of bitterness? Still allowing past enemies to control your mood or self-confidence? Are you still mad at God for allowing your loved one to be taken too soon? Do you ever daydream about what your life would be like if things hadn't changed, if people had kept their promises, if you knew *then* what you know *now*?

Don't let your tight and tired grip on yesterday choke the blessings of today. Most of the time, we're afraid to let go – afraid we'll forget the good times or never escape the bad times. Letting go doesn't erase painful memories, but it declaws its power to shred your joy. You won't embrace *what is*, if you can't let go of *what was*. Whether it was an ugly break-up or a dream that crumbled in failure, within you is the God-given power to loosen your grip on the past and let go of what's lost. Whether you're trying to honor someone's memory or punish your haters, you won't experience freedom until you accept your losses and surrender to God what's left...of your family, of your dreams, of *you*.

If God allowed you to lose something, you ultimately didn't need it to fulfill your purpose in the world. Now it's time for me to mention one of the most cliché scriptures in the Bible. But give it a chance to speak to you again. Romans 8:28 says, *"And we know that all things work together for good to those who love God, to those who are the called according to His purpose."* This verse is powerful and brings encouragement to the soul. No matter what hardship you are going through right now, God is going to see you through it. Often times we get lost in the fog of worry and feel like God has forgotten about our pain or condition. We feel as though Jesus has overlooked our situation. But the reality is, He's closer to you than you realize and His hand is at work in your life. This is God's way of soothing our worries and reminding us that He is in charge, even when life is spinning out of control. Your divine destiny encompasses all of life's experiences—both good and bad. Allow me to explain this verse.

"All things" means that every experience, even if not fully understood, fits somewhere into God's master plan.

"Work together" carries the idea that your life's experiences and events function together like gears in a clock. God devises means and works undercover to fulfill His purpose in your life.

"For the good" are three words we struggle to wrap our minds around when the *things* that happened were painful. How can something positive flow from pain or dysfunction? The truth behind "for the good" is that our experiences are not wasted. Your pain was not in vain.

"Those who love God" classifies the group of people who know Jesus intimately. This verse doesn't apply to every human being. It will not bring comfort to those who continue to reject Jesus and His grace. These promises are directed towards the church—God's beloved sons and daughters. Now, I know we all say we love God. However, just saying *you love Him* isn't enough. In John 14:21, Jesus said, *"He who has My commandments*

and keeps them, it is he who loves Me..." No matter what you've been told, the truth is that loving God is a lifestyle, a daily decision of obedience. Nothing tells God that you love Him more than when you obey His Word, follow His counsel, and walk in holy fear. Sound crazy? Not really, when you consider that love is a behavior, not just an emotion.

"To those who are called according to His purpose" is a phrase that clarifies who benefits the most from God's sovereign plans. The key here is "His" purpose. Again, Paul is saying that things will work out well for those who are living and walking in His purpose for their lives. Being in the will of God affects how you handle adversity. On the same token, being in His purpose doesn't negate hardship either. It gives God greater access to move on your behalf, because your faith is in Him and you've surrendered to His Lordship.

Moving forward isn't always about finding closure, but finding openings. Could it be that God is opening a door in front of you, but you're too distracted to see it?

CUT THE ROPE

Don't suppress your emotions or questions, but surrender them to God so that you're free to embrace the present. Letting go of what's lost is possible when you realize that your entire life is secure in God's hands—that what you release in faith, you will gain in victory. Let Jesus be Lord over what you've lost and what you've got left. A lot of people are torn between their past and their future. They feel like a rope in a game of *tug of war*, pulled in opposing directions. Just when you feel you're making progress and getting ahead, the past will jolt you back into a place of neutrality or disillusionment.

Rattled with frustration, and confused with everyone's opinions, you begin to accept defeat. But you can end this tiresome game of tug of war by simply cutting the rope with the sharp edge of God's Word. There doesn't need to be a constant tension of past vs. future when you embrace the present and walk by faith. Regret over the past, and worry over the future, lead to a miserable life.

It's also possible that you're the only one pulling the rope back and forth, even though you're blaming everything on the devil. Part of you is pulling yourself back with carnal thinking, uncontrolled emotions, or unforgiveness, and the other part of you is pulling yourself forward with hopes and dreams of tomorrow. Instead of enjoying the prime of your life, you're still tangled up in a rope of past vs. future.

The apostle Paul wrote, *"Brethren, I do not count myself to have apprehended; but one thing I do, forgetting those things which are behind and reaching forward to those things which are ahead, I press toward the goal for the prize of the upward call of God in Christ Jesus"* (Philippians 3:13-14). The secret to cutting the rope of past-vs.-future is to let go of what's behind you and reach forward to what's right in front of you. Paul was honest about his journey. If I could rewrite Paul's words with some creative license, I would say the following:

First of all, I haven't arrived yet. I can't act like I'm there, because I'm not. But one thing is for sure; I'm not dwelling on my past or *allowing it to pull me backwards. What happened **to** me ultimately happened for me. That includes the good, the bad, and the ugly. Going back in time is not an option. Therefore, I choose to focus all my energy on the things ahead of me. I consume myself with God and His purpose for my life. Please excuse all the scaffolding around me; I'm still under construction. I'm still a work in progress. But thankfully I've got the blueprints! I've got radical faith, but also practical wisdom. Through grace, I'm pressing ahead without rushing. I won't panic because I'm getting closer, climbing higher and dreaming bigger. My direction is forward and my calling is upward in Christ Jesus.*

Just as a side note: A lot of people are satisfied with false progress, like running on a treadmill, they burn time and energy going nowhere. Genuine delay is always better than fake progress. At least you're not lying to yourself. You can't start building from where you wish you were, but only from where you actually are. God will always take you back to the lesson you skipped. Save yourself further heartache and get honest about where you are—emotionally, financially, or spiritually. Then take action. Until then, progress will only be a wish and never a reality.

Cut the tension between your past and future by letting go of what's lost and lifting up to God what's left. The leftovers are not trash. Don't throw away your dreams because you think what's left is unusable. God sees value in places where we usually give up. He knows something about resurrecting dead things and raising up new life. Jesus *is* the Resurrection and the Life. Besides, if you feel there's nothing left worth fighting for, what have you got to lose by surrendering all to Christ?

Stop debating with yourself and cut the rope. Decide right now that you're going to live in the moment and trust God to take you to places you can't even imagine.

LIFT UP WHAT'S LEFT

Like Moses, maybe you're holding the ashes of what's left of your heart and your hopes. Oftentimes, we want to hold onto what's left and lock it away. When our funds are low, there is a strong urge to withhold our offerings and tithes because doubt creeps into our spirit and whispers, "If you give, you won't have anything left." When offended by someone, there is a voice that says, "If you forgive him, it says that you're okay with what was done." When you've tried and failed a few times, you hear "Don't try again. It's not worth it."

Stop listening to those voices of doubt and fear! You serve a God who specializes in using what's left to perform miracles. God told Moses what to do with the ashes: *"scatter it toward the heavens in the sight of Pharaoh"* (Exodus 9:8). This verse unlocks a few insights which I think you should consider and apply to your life. First, Moses lifted what was left to *heaven*. The Hebrew word for "heaven" in this text isn't a reference to the celestial city. The original word denotes "sky" or "air."

However, the spiritual symbolism implies that God will bless what we lift up. If you will raise your brokenness or cares in worship, God will demonstrate His power in your life. I'm reminded of these words in 1 Peter 5:7: *"cast all your cares upon Him, for He cares for you."*

The Greek word for "casting" is *epirito*, which means, "*to throw or cast upon.*" Don't just softly hand over your worries and cares to God, but launch them upward! Aim high and release the ashes of what's left in the Name of Jesus! Whatever is left of your dreams, lift it up to God. He will use the ashes of your trials if you throw it heavenward in worship.

Secondly, Moses lifted what was left before his enemy, Pharaoh. Even your enemies will realize the miracle of what's left! God used the lifted ashes to spread a plague over the Egyptians, causing boils to break out on their skins. Verse 11 says the magicians and their spells could not stand before Moses because of the boils. I got news for the devil; God will use what's left of your faith to break every curse and evil scheme over your life. There is a miracle hidden in what's left.

Will you respond to God's call to trust Him and hope again? Maybe you're looking at your life and don't feel you have enough faith, enough strength, enough money, or enough time to see a miracle. God's strength is not perfected in your strengths, but in your weaknesses. According to Isaiah 61:3, God gives His people "*beauty for ashes.*" He takes the ashes of what's left of our lives, our hopes, and our dreams, and creates something beautiful.

As I wrote previously, ash is what's left after something has burned. I would like to shift gears in this chapter and describe three specific ways that ashes become beautiful.

1. Ashes become beautiful when they Signify Repentance

In the Bible, ashes may also represent repentance. Jesus said in

Matthew 11:21, *"Woe to you, Chorazin! Woe to you, Bethsaida! For if the mighty works which were done in you had been done in Tyre and Sidon, they would have repented long ago in sackcloth and ashes."* Jesus rebuked the two cities of Chorazin and Bethsaida because they had experienced the power of God, but did not turn their hearts to Him. They were touched, healed, and set free, but refused to repent of their sins. They went from experience to experience, service to service (so to speak), but never fully surrendered their lives to Christ.

The citizens of these two cities enjoyed God's presence, but wouldn't let go of their sinful lifestyle. All those miracles and moments with Jesus should have produced ashes of repentance. Could it be that God is waiting on you to repent and turn to Him? Maybe He's looking for ashes of repentance? If you haven't repented of your sins, the time is now. God will give you beauty for ashes.

2. Ashes become beautiful when they Renew your Faith

I'm reminded of something that Job did after losing everything he loved and suffering from painful blisters on this body. Job 2:8 says, *"Then Job took a piece of broken pottery and scraped himself with it as he sat among the ashes."* This disturbing picture reveals a man who's trying to find relief from both the open sores on his skin, and the emotional sores in his heart. But I also find his location interesting. Why was Job sitting in a pile of ashes? Maybe I can shed some light on this.

Job used to continually offer burnt sacrifices to God, which was an act of devotion and worship. But since he had lost all his cattle and sheep, he had nothing to sacrifice on his altar. In essence, Job lost his form of worship. His life could not express the type of sacrificial praise he was accustomed to. Therefore, all Job could do was go back to the place where he used to encounter God and sit on the ashes — to remind him of God's presence. When you're in a trial and feel like you have nothing left, you may have to reach back to where you first kindled a relationship with God. For me, sometimes I go back to my old Bible, that's faded and falling apart, and read my highlighted verses from many years ago. It sparks a hunger in me and reminds me of simpler days gone by. Sometimes I'll sing an older Gospel hymn that transports me back in time and reminds me of how faithful God has been throughout the years. Then there are times I'll just remember the first time I felt God's presence at an altar or received the Holy Ghost.

I know I talk a lot about not living in the past, but there are moments when you need to remember God's faithfulness in order to rekindle your faith in the present. When you remember from where He brought you, or delivered you, or what you felt when you first encountered His love, those ashes can reignite your spirit. Sometimes it's just the busyness of lives which snuff out the flame of passion. Our worship can gradually become mechanical or ice-cold with predictability. God told the Ephesian church, despite all their good works, *"Nevertheless I have this against you, that you have left your first love"* (Revelation 2:4). Sometimes we forget our first love for God, and need to reach back until we burn with passion again.

As you sit in the ashes, your desire can be rekindled, your

hope can be restored, and your faith can be renewed!

3. Ashes become beautiful when they Fuel your Purpose

There's an unusual verse found Numbers 19:9 that refers to an Old Testament purification process. It reads: *"A man who is clean shall gather up the ashes of the heifer and put them in a ceremonially clean place outside the camp. They are to be kept by the Israelite community for use in the water of cleansing; it is for purification from sin."* This law is no longer practiced, but the spiritual principle remains. The real blessing was not found in the living animal, but in its ashes. Your miracle is in what you have left, after the fiery trial stops burning. Whatever the fire, the trial, took from you wasn't necessary to fulfill *your* destiny. Otherwise, God would have never allowed it to burn up. God uses what you have left.

Whatever you do, don't throw away your ashes. God will turn them into something beautiful. He'll use them to fuel your future.

He'll turn your mistakes into miracles.

He'll turn your wounds into wonders.

God wants to turn your ashes into a beautiful life.

{Chapter 6}

Singing in the Rain

I f there was a vote for "The Most Impractical Command in the New Testament," or "The Verse Most Likely to Frustrate You," I would nominate what the apostle Paul said in 1 Thessalonians 5:18. Now before you read it and think I've lost my mind, let me say that I don't disagree with what it says. I affirm this scripture without dispute. I preach it and believe it. Which is why I've struggled to live up to its implications. Here's what it says, *"in everything give thanks; for this is the will of God in Christ Jesus for you."* Seems pretty simple at first glance. In fact, you might not consider this verse impractical in the least bit. But when you're in a deep cave of pain or disappointment, this verse clashes against your sensibilities on every level. Paul's command sounds like a great theory or easy exercise, until I was cradling my 3-pound baby girl in that cold hospital room, as she clung faintly to life.

Certain commands look great on paper. They make great sound bites. They feel wonderful when you're riding on cloud nine – when everyone is healthy, the paychecks are rolling, and it's the second day of your Hawaiian vacation. Thanksgiving is easy to do when the blessings are pouring down and you're puddle-jumping in success. But it takes everything within your soul when trials are raining down and those puddles feel like oceans. Let me reassure you that God's word is not working *against* you, but *for* you. Paul, a man who suffered greatly for the cause of Christ, shared the secret to surviving the storms of life, to changing the tune of our attitude against all reason. Notice what Paul does not say. He does not say, *"**for** everything give thanks."* Rather, *"**in** everything give thanks."*

We are not called to thank God *for* our circumstances, but to thank God *through* our circumstances. You don't need to thank God *for* your sickness, but *in* and *through* your sickness. God isn't calling you to thank Him *for* your unpaid bills, but *through* the process of paying them. You don't need to thank God *for* your injustices, but *through* them. Your situation does not have to improve for your gratitude and praise to increase.

An attitude of gratitude is cultivated in the seasons of life where you have to dig deep and find reasons to be thankful, where you look for the silver lining in your storm clouds. And if the puddles feel like oceans, maybe it's time to swim.

MAKE IT A MUSICAL

I have to admit that I'm not a big fan of musicals. That's

probably an understatement. Truth is, they drive me crazy. I can't sit for an hour or more watching people dance and sing around on stage. For years, my wife and I have wanted to go see *The Lion King* on Broadway. I know the show is great. I believe the reviews. I trust my friend's opinions. But I just can't seem to get motivated to go. One time we even stayed at a hotel directly across from *The Lion King* Theater in Times Square, New York, and *still* didn't make it happen. I know, epic fail.

Despite my dislike of musicals, I, like many musical and non-musical people have heard of the 1952 film, *Singin' in the Rain*. This American musical classic follows the journey of a fictitious Hollywood couple, Don Lockwood and Lina Lamont, whose lives are turned upside down as they attempt to reinvent their careers from silent film actors to talking actors. In the film, the studio executives want to turn their latest production into a talking film, but everything that can go wrong does go wrong. Their solution: *make it a musical.* When they mixed in singing and dancing, their worst fears turn into a golden opportunity. Don and Kathy live happily ever after.

Author Vivian Greene once said, *"Life isn't about waiting for the storm to pass...it's about learning to dance in the rain."* I would slightly alter that to say, "it's about learning to *sing* in the rain." Instead of complaining or allowing your struggles to define you, *make it a musical.* That's a choice the Israelites faced during one of their darkest periods. The scene is found in Psalm 137:1-4: *"By the rivers of Babylon we sat down; there we wept when we remembered Zion. On the willows nearby we hung up our harps. Those who captured us told us to sing; they told us to entertain them:" Sing us a song about Zion." How can we sing a song to the Lord in a strange land?"*

These are the words of a people who were taken captive by the armies of Babylon. Their beloved city, Jerusalem, had been ravaged and burned. Suddenly, they were brought into a strange land, an unfamiliar place. Then, adding insult to injury, the Israelites were mocked by their captors to sing a song. They replied with a question: *"How can we sing a song to the Lord in a strange land?"* Similar questions can appear our own lives:

How can I sing to God...when my life is filled with frustrations?

How can I sing to God...when my spirit feels so dry?

How can I sing to God...while commuting to a dead-end job?

...after signing divorce papers?

...after a negative medical prognosis?

I don't think the Israelites' question was a response to their captors. In fact, it sounds more introspective, as if they were asking themselves a rhetorical question. But honestly, haven't you ever felt that way? Like, what's the point? How can I lift my heart in praise, when my world is crumbling around me? It's a question that puzzles us in the strange land of frustration and disappointment. The Word of God commands us to praise Him, but that doesn't always fit into our reality.

Then again, maybe that's why scripture *commands* it, not suggests it—because God knows our tendency to base our praise on how we feel and what our circumstances are saying to us. The Israelites displayed their grief with a silence protest. They hung their harps on the willow trees. The strings of the harps were wrapped tightly on the branches and left to hang like lifeless ornaments. They were in no mood to play their instruments and sing praises to God. Let's be fair in our criticism. It's not like they were upset about a Facebook post from an ex-boyfriend or a flat tire on the way to church. They were ripped from their homes and stuck in a miserable place. Nevertheless, their enemies did not take their harps. Somehow in their struggle, they still possessed the ability to sing praises to God. No matter what you go through in life, the devil cannot rob you of your ability to praise God. Whether you choose to praise Him or not, is entirely up to you. But as with the Israelites, you have control over your harp. I'm not saying it's easy or that you'll feel the same each day, but you can keep your harp tuned with an attitude of praise.

There are some powerful word pictures in Psalm 137.

- Harps represent praise and joy.
- Willows represent struggle and pain.
- The strange land represents the unfamiliar and uncertain.

It's in the strange places of life, the willows, that we tend to hang up our harps of praise. Don't base your song on where you are, but on where *God is* and what He says about you. Don't let your willows silence your praise. Instead, turn your willows into songs of praise. There's an unusual verse found in Leviticus 23:40 that says, *"On the first day you are to take branches from luxuriant trees—from palms, willows and other leafy trees—and rejoice before the Lord your God for seven days."* God was telling His people, bring your willow branches (your struggles and hurts) into my presence and rejoice. As Christ-followers, we're not called to rejoice *because* of pain, but to rejoice *in spite* of pain. When dreams shatter and you feel like giving up, God calls us to bring our brokenness into His presence. In Philippians 4:4, we are told to, *"Rejoice in the Lord always. Again I will say, rejoice!"*

The apostle Paul knew that the first sentence in that verse would jolt us. *Surely he doesn't mean "always."* So he doubles down. *"Again I will say, rejoice!"*

If you're going to survive the troubles you're facing, you must learn how to praise God when there are willows in your life, when it's pouring problems. Make it a musical. Get your iPhone music player or old-school CD player and sing along with songs of worship, with spiritual hymns that will attract the presence of God and strengthen your spirit. Or simply sing whatever praise song you know and get lost in God's atmosphere. Paul didn't just pen that verse because it sounded nice. I'm sure he remembered the night that he and Silas were imprisoned in the city of Philippi, all because he set a young woman free from demonic oppression.

While sitting in the deepest, darkest cell in the prison, *"at midnight Paul and Silas were praying and singing hymns to God, and the prisoners were listening to them"* (Acts 16:25). Paul and Silas had a choice to make. They could either be like the Israelites who hung up their praise, or they could sing and praise God in spite of their dark moment.

What happened next was nothing short of a jailhouse rock: *"Suddenly there was a great earthquake, so that the foundations of the prison were shaken; and immediately all the doors were opened and everyone's chains were loosed"* (Acts 16:26). There is power in praise! When you begin to activate your mouth in praise, something begins to change in the spiritual realm. As God is glorified, your enemy is horrified. This level of praise confuses Satan and his cronies. They cannot fathom how a suffering human can continue to offer up praises to God when all hell is breaking loose.

When a person has been dealt one blow after another and still magnifies God, there is a supernatural shift. If those prison walls that held Paul and Silas could talk, I'm sure they would testify, *"Nothing like this has ever happened before! No one has been able to break our hold onto his life. We were made to detain and punish the worst people. But when these two men started singing songs to their God, we felt the earth shake and foundations wobble! We tried to tighten our grip, but to no avail. As they lifted their voices, we broke apart."*

The praise of a broken heart touches the heart of God and creates a sound like no other. The Lord is drawn to the scent of worship that, against all logic, still finds reason to bless His Name—an attitude of gratitude that outweighs the pain. There may be nothing more precious to God than the sound of a wounded worshipper, whose shattered heart becomes the wind chimes of heaven.

SONGS IN THE NIGHT

"Songbirds are taught to sing in the dark, and we are put into the shadow of God's hand until we learn to hear Him."
- Oswald Chambers

The song you sing in life's shadows cannot be replicated in anywhere else in creation. Even the angelic choirs of heaven cannot understand or experience the pain behind our songs. I'm reminded of Job's young friend, Elihu, who told him that the Lord *"gives songs in the night"* (Job 35:10). Elihu had a great point—or more accurately—a revelation. *God writes songs for us...when our song is gone.* He fills the dead space of our lives with heavenly vibrations and rhythms. We are tempted to hang our harps on the willows. And perhaps, for a moment, we do.

Some days we just don't feel it. Some nights our hearts sit in silence. But don't let your worship get tangled in the willows of frustration! God has written songs on our hearts, melodies that tune our lives to His divine intentions, worship that harmonizes with heaven's symphony. Your night song is not "your" song, but the song that God wrote to Himself when your life couldn't find the right tune. God does this because He still desires and deserves our worship. And our hearts are made stronger and wiser in the process.

Songs in the night are not the product of emotion, but of revelation. We're not talking about heaven's version of the "the blues," melancholic music that's born from human pain. Emotion is a passenger, not the driver. Ultimately it's the Holy Spirit that is filling up your worship, a deep that calls unto deep, an innermost melody that in some cases—words cannot capture.

GOD'S SOUNDTRACKS

In Paul's letter to the Ephesian church, he wrote, *"speaking to one another in psalms and hymns and spiritual songs, singing and making melody in your heart to the Lord, giving thanks always for all things to God the Father in the name of our Lord Jesus Christ"* (5:19-20). This passage is lifted from chapter five where Paul is describing how we should walk through life as children of God. It's interesting that in this section dealing with growing in wisdom, Paul seems to venture off-script to reassert the power of worship. But maybe there is an unseen correlation between wisdom and worship. Maybe worship *reveals* our wisdom (it takes wisdom to recognize God's presence) and also *increases* our wisdom (the closer God is, the greater He influences our decisions). What are clear from Paul's writings are two directions of worship that bring hope. I view these as God's soundtracks. Let's unpack them and see what value they hold.

1. Horizontal Worship

You would think in a passage about singing to God that Paul would begin *with God*. He doesn't. One focus of our singing is not God, but *one another*. Now, please don't think to yourself "blasphemy!" Paul is not suggesting that we "worship one another," but rather "address one another or encourage one another with worship." There is a huge difference. Through corporate worship we are declaring God's Word to one another through psalms, hymns, and spiritual songs – for the purpose of proclaiming truth and ministering to one another. God is glorified, and the church is edified. Through the medium of songs, we're being taught by our brothers and sisters to trust in the Lord.

Worship not only touches the heart of God, but it touches the heart of the worshipper. Something powerful happens to us as a result of proclaimed praise and glory to God. A few pages ago, we read where Paul and Silas sang praises in the prison. There's no doubt they were singing *to* God, but their praise caught the attention of the prisoners in the cells: *"at midnight Paul and Silas were praying and singing hymns to God, and the prisoners were listening to them"* (Acts 16:25). The prisoners who were bound couldn't help but listen to the songs and be filled with hope. Paul and Silas weren't preaching or teaching, but their song echoed down the dungeon halls, into the hearts of those despondent men. As they sang aloud and worshipped our almighty God, *"all the doors were opened and everyone's chains were loosed."*

Did you catch that?

Not only did Paul and Silas get free, but everyone in their proximity got free. The prisoners didn't sing one note or even clap their hands, yet their shackles were broken and their chains were loosed. That's the power of horizontal worship! You never know how your worship will affect another. And you never know how another's worship will affect you.

This is one of many reasons why I attend church every Sunday. As we gather for worship and hear sounds of praise, things in my life have the potential to shift – things I cannot move or break with my own human strength. When I see someone praising God joyfully, whose condition or pain may be worse than mine, it lifts my spirit and leaves me without an excuse. Suddenly, my hope rises. My faith feeds off the worship of my brothers and sisters.

I can relate to the lyrics of David, who told the Lord, *"... You shall surround me with songs of deliverance"* (Psalm 32:7). God protects you with His songs. He surrounds you with a war cry of worship that repels your adversary. This truth correlates with the words of the prophet Zephaniah: *"...He will rejoice over you with singing"* (3:17). Can you imagine a God who literally celebrates over you with songs of joy? So many of us have missed this beautiful picture of God's love. The literal sound of God's singing voice must be astonishing and indescribable; I imagine it records on scales unknown to human ears, unattainable with man-made instruments. How majestic His song must be! Oh!

how the angels must stand in awe and the heavens gaze with amazement. Oh! how the silence of eternity and the stars are broken at the enchanting hymns of the Almighty God!

And…it is all over you, surrounding you, His beloved child.

Creation doesn't make Him sing. The angels don't make Him sing. But one look at you, His redeemed child, causes Him to open His mouth and sing His solo. Friend, that ought to make you smile with tears of joy. No matter how bad your situation is and what frustrations you're battling, there is a transcendent peace with knowing that your Savior serenades your soul. You are not alone.

However, maybe you're wondering where you can download God's songs on iTunes or why you haven't heard any celestial music playing in the background of your daily life. I believe this soundtrack of hope is connected to the voices of the church. In other words, God transfers His songs into His minstrels, His worshippers, and then surrounds us as they sing and play their instruments.

In the same way that the Holy Spirit inspires a preacher with a message from the Word and speaks through him, the Holy Spirit inspires minstrels with songs that draw the presence of God and dispels our fears. For instance, whenever a distressing spirit would trouble King Saul, He would summon David to his palace to play his harp. The Bible says, *"And so it was, whenever the spirit from God was upon Saul, that David would take a harp and play it with his hand. Then Saul would become refreshed and well, and the distressing spirit would depart from him"* (1 Samuel 16:23). When you get in an atmosphere of horizontal worship, there is a refreshing spirit that energizes your soul. The Holy Spirit sings *through* His worshippers.

2. Vertical Worship

The next soundtrack that Paul affirms is vertical worship: *"singing and making melody in your heart to the Lord"* (Ephesians 5:19). Here, Paul identifies only one benefactor—the Lord Himself. This dimension of worship is intimate and personal. It's between you and God. We hear so much nowadays on the subject of worship, and it seems like everybody has their own opinion about what it is, how to do it, and of course, why we do it. Volumes of books have been written about worship and how we should understand it. Even the book you're holding right now is laced with thoughts and precepts on worship. The topic of worship is deep and wide. So, as I pondered on Ephesians 5:19, I wanted to find something unique to this text. What I discovered is that Paul is not talking about audible worship through the use of our voices, bodies, or instruments. Notice: he teaches us to *sing and make melody in our hearts,* not only with our voices, but with inward affection. Worship is mostly associated with audible sounds. But there is a deeper level of worship that God yearns for.

Your worship is unique; it is distinctively *you*. No one else can replace your worship because God made you an original. He doesn't want to hear "a" song. He wants to hear "your" song. He longs to hear your thoughts of love, the thirst of your heart – like the deer pants for streams of water. The Father seeks true worshippers. He wants to awaken your heart to love and adoration, to an intimate relationship with Jesus. Worship is more than a song; it's a disposition of the heart, a life that delights in the Lord and seeks the thrill of His daily presence. To make melody in your heart is to worship from within. It is to *"set your affection on things above, not on things on the earth"*

(Colossians 3:2). But it goes beyond your set time of daily devotion and prayer. According to Paul, this vein of worship is about having a worshipful mindset that hosts God's presence and lives with an awareness of Him.

What you magnify, you magnetize.

The more you magnify and worship God, the more of His presence you will attract. Conversely, if you magnify your worries, your worries will snowball over your life. If you worship your wounds by constantly focusing on them, by blaming others and holding grudges, your emotional bleeding will perpetuate. If you magnify your disagreements with people, it will attract more feuds. For this reason we must prioritize the presence of God and worship Him as a lifestyle. In doing so, your life will magnetically draw more of His presence. The Bible says, *"Draw near to God and He will draw near to you…"* (James 4:8). This is our daily call: to incline our hearts towards the presence of God and maintain an awareness of Him. This doesn't mean we walk around like spiritual zombies or seclude ourselves in a monastery high in the mountains. It means that we are mindful of the Holy Spirit and engage with Him daily. It means living for His pleasure, not our own. It means following His lead and keeping Him close. Whatever you do, don't lose sight of His presence. Don't forget God. There's actually a frightening example in the gospels of someone who did. You might be surprised to know who it was.

MISSING JESUS

In the Gospel of Luke chapter two, Mary and Joseph had taken their 12-year-old son Jesus to Jerusalem for the Passover festival.

Every male Jew living within a reasonable distance of Jerusalem was required to be there for this annual holiday. So Mary and Joseph, and all their family and friends from Nazareth, made the arduous journey. When Passover ended, Mary and Joseph packed up and headed home. But after many hours of traveling, something didn't feel right. Mary swiveled her head to the left and to the right. Then she must have spun herself around and darted her eyes to the back of the convoy.

"Something is not right." She whispered to herself.

From one second to the next, panic froze the blood in her veins.

"Joseph!" Mary cried with bated breath. *"Where is Jesus? Please tell me you know where he is!"* The blank look on Joseph's face said it all. Somehow, somewhere, the most important person in the world went missing and was nowhere to be found. Mary and Joseph immediately saddled their belongings and rushed back to Jerusalem. Their fears pulsated as they searched the city for two days, retracing their steps and asking around. Every promising lead went ice cold. But at last, on the third day the search party was called off. Mary and Joseph had finally found Jesus in the temple. This frightening story reminds us of how easy it is to lose sight of Jesus. It begs to wonder, if Mary, the mother of Jesus, could lose sight of His presence, then who am I? If Mary lost Jesus (for three days), then I am just as capable of losing sight of His presence in my life. This incident is a cautionary tale that suggests at least three lessons for us to consider.

1. You can lose Him and not know it
The Bible tells us, *"Jesus lingered behind in Jerusalem. And Joseph*

and His mother did not know it" (Luke 2:43). Mary went a whole day before she realized that Jesus wasn't there. It is possible to lose sight of Jesus and not even know it. Here's the thing, though. It wasn't like Mary was trying to lose Jesus. She didn't wake up that morning with intentions to leave Jesus behind in Jerusalem. She merely let her guard down and got too comfortable with life as usual. As verse 44 reveals, *"supposing Him to have been in the company, they went a day's journey."* Perhaps Mary and Joseph made some false assumptions that we're prone to make ourselves sometimes. Two immediately come to mind.

First, there is *religious assumption,* which says, *"I attended a spiritual event, I suppose Jesus is with me."* Mary and Joseph were highly dutiful and devoted to Judaism. And this story finds them fresh off a spiritual pilgrimage to their holy city. *But they still lost Jesus.* Let me just say that although attending church is a great custom to have, it is not a guaranteed blessing. Frankly, it's what you do when you're at church that counts, not simply showing up. Too often we feel validated just for being in attendance on Sunday, but fail to benefit from an enriching encounter with God. We walk out the same way we walk in. Or, more concerning, we engage with Jesus' presence at church but then leave Him there as we exit the building.

Next, there is *historical assumption,* which says, *"I've known Jesus for a long time, I suppose He is with me."* Nobody knew Jesus like Mary did. She was His mother. But that familiarity with Jesus also made their relationship susceptible to routine and ordinariness. Simply put, Jesus *could* get lost in the mix of daily life and start blending in with everything else, and everyone else. In Mary's case, Jesus could become too common. But that's a pitfall someone must avoid when you've grown up in church or have served the Lord for a long time. There is a real temptation to become stagnant and rest on past experiences. The longer you have something, the easier it is to take it for granted. The message here is that we have to stay connected to God and not allow religious clutter or daily routines to distract us from the highest calling of our lives – to worship and know Him intimately.

The second lesson we see from this ordeal will be both painfully obvious and obviously painful.

2. You can find Him, right where you left Him

After realizing that Jesus was missing, Mary and Joseph's first reaction wasn't necessarily bad. On the surface, it made perfect sense. They began looking for Jesus *"...among their relatives and acquaintances"* (Luke 2:44). I'm not knocking them for that. This seemed like a logical place to start. But once their initial search came up empty, it was clear that this wasn't going to be a quick fix. They would have to change their plans entirely. You won't find Jesus by looking where it's most convenient or comfortable. When you're grasping for more of His presence, it's going to cost you.

Verse 45 says, *"So when they did not find Him, they returned to Jerusalem, seeking Him."* Mary had Jesus at the temple in Jerusalem, but lost track of Him on the way home. Likewise, there are so many people nowadays who know Jesus in the temple, but lose Him on the way home. You can lose Jesus on the way home...

...When you fail to trust Him.

...When you forget what His Word told you.

...When you don't forgive the person who offended you.

…When you avoid honesty about your struggles.

Your journey towards greatness in God starts where you left off. God will always lead you back to the process you skipped, the places where you gave up, the people whom you hurt, the sin you covered up, the business you left unfinished, the promise you didn't keep, the wound you left unhealed, the lesson you left unlearned, the bill you left unpaid, the dream you left unfulfilled, the song you didn't sing, or the message you didn't live.

Do you want to know where God is?

He's right where you left Him.

There (and only there) will you find Him. We need to realize that sometimes you don't get to crumple-up the paper and start over until you meet God at the place where you left Him. Until then, you're only playing the part and wasting precious time. Pick up where you left off!

Let's look at the third lesson from this scene. Here we discover that God reveals His plan through our pain, and why there is reason to sing in the rain!

3. Your frustrations are God's invitations

Once Mary found her missing Son, she realized that He was never lost. It was the reverse. Mary and Joseph were lost, because Jesus was exactly where He needed to be. Of course, in the moment, it was a desperate and emotional reunion. After squeezing Jesus in her shaken arms and sprinkling his head with teardrops, Mary then collected her thoughts, cleared her throat and stooped down eye-to-eye with her son. What ensued was a scolding that takes me back thirty years to my own childhood, when my gentle mom would morph into a drill sergeant when my brothers and I got out of hand. I knew, once I got that certain look, I was busted! I imagine Mary had a similar look and tone when she said, *"Son, why have You done this to us? Look, Your father and I have sought You anxiously"* (Luke 2:48). Notice that Mary's first reaction was to *blame Jesus* for her frustrations. And I think perhaps that the writer, Luke, only gave us the Reader's Digest version of Mary's complaint. If captured on raw video, I'm sure we would hear Mary say something to the effect of:

"Jesus! Son! Where have you been all this time? Why didn't you tell us where you were going? I've been worried sick about you for the past three days, thinking that maybe somebody kidnapped you or worse, killed you! You were supposed to stay close to us. We've had this discussion many times already. Son, we love you and are so relieved we found you, but look at the trouble you caused. Your father and I haven't been able to sleep or eat because we've been so anxious to find you. Why would you put us through this trouble? Why have you done this to us?"

My version of Mary's scolding might not be biblically accurate, but it's 100% humanly accurate. It's also how many of us feel when life disappoints. We tend to blame God. But allow me to adjust your perspective. Could it be that the frustrations meant to destroy you, can actually push you closer to Jesus? Is it possible that God is using your struggle or pain to draw you into a tighter relationship with Him?

Problems rain. But keep singing.

Willows grow. But keep worshipping.

We lose our way. But keep searching for Him.

Life is filled with disappointments and struggles. But it does no good to blame God, to blame yourself or to even blame the devil (which is our default). God is not causing all your struggles, but He intends to use them to drive you into His arms of grace. He intends to get glory out of your life. Verse 46 says, *"after three days they found Him."* I have a hunch that after this experience, Mary and Jesus' relationship changed. She would never leave Him out-of-sight again. She might have realized that it wasn't really His fault, that she should have been more vigilant. Either way, her frustrations became God's invitations to search for Him in a greater way—to pursue His presence at all costs.

Orient your heart towards God in worship, regardless of the adversities you face. Because ultimately that's where you find Him and the hope He gives.

{Chapter 7}

Rejection is Redirection

iddle school and high school were challenging years for me. Like many teenagers, I struggled to find where I fit in with everyone else. I craved acceptance from my peers. I guess that's part of growing up for a lot of us. I thought if I dressed like them, talked like them and listened to their kind of music, they would eventually accept me. On top of that, I battled with insecurities about my physical appearance and did everything I could to hide my blemishes. Again, pretty normal for a teenager. But my quest for social acceptance came with the added pressure of being a pastor's kid and church members expecting you to be a perfect little angel.

In Middle school, I started tagging (graffiti art). Even

though I had some real artistic talent, I was more concerned with using it to fit in with the right crowds. I thought I finally found my place, but then my "friends" were the ones who sold me out after I tagged in some school buildings. Of course, it was really foolish of me to vandalize school property. Not a proud moment of mine. I deserved to be caught and punished. But I also learned that my so-called friends willingly offered-up my name to school officials and never had my back. Basically, I wasn't one of them.

At the time, I didn't know how to express myself to those who could help me. After being suspended a week from school, I had a chance to explain my actions. My dad and I drove away from the principal's office. *Here it comes,* I thought. *I'm dead.* But his tone of voice was different than I expected, especially after being forced to pay a fine and hearing that I might be expelled three weeks before graduation. I was expecting to be grilled harshly or even spanked like a child again. Instead my dad looked over at me with a puzzled and worried face and asked, *"Jacob, why are you doing this? What is your problem?"* I just sat there silent—unable to explain myself. I didn't know what was wrong with me. All I knew was that when I came back to school, my "friends" would be laughing at me.

Sports didn't boost my confidence much either. I played two years of high school football and could never earn a starting spot. So the jocks didn't let me in their inner circle. Again, ousted.

I did have some height and a passion for basketball. *Maybe this is my place,* I thought to myself. But on the first day of tryouts, I broke my foot during a pick-up game—*before* tryouts had even started! I left home with a huge bulge on my left foot the size of a tennis ball and felt like such a loser. The next day I arrived to school in crutches with a cast. That might as well be the proverbial symbol of how I felt as a teenager—rejected.

Rejected by my friends.

Rejected by my teammates.

Rejected by those I wanted to impress.

I wasn't bad enough for the bad boys. I wasn't good enough for the goody two-shoes. That period of my life was scary. It was like I was fighting shifting shadows and only hurting myself. At one point I became so frustrated that I would throw fits of rage in my room—punching the walls and growling under my breath. I would wait until I was home alone because I didn't want to alarm my parents. Needless to say, nobody knew how much I was struggling. I guess I hid it well. When left alone, it was like a time bomb went off in my head. I even remember going to church, having so much hatred building inside of me, that I couldn't bare to even look at some people in their eyes.

It's hard for me to write about this stuff. I've had to stop a few times just to take a deep breath and start typing again. I rarely open up about these things. And many of my long-time friends and family don't even know how I struggled because I bottled it up so tightly. But so much of these frustrations resulted from the rejection that I perceived.

Not until my senior year of high school did I really allow the Lord to start changing my heart. I began to realize that I was never able to fit in because He called me for something much greater. And it wasn't until adulthood did I see that behind all that rejection was God's providential grace at work in me. I've discovered that *rejection is nothing more than redirection.*

I know it sounds like a contradiction. How could rejection produce something positive? But as I began to study the life of Christ, it changed the way I processed rejection and allowed me to keep it all in perspective. Your experience with rejection might be different than mine or much worse than mine. Your life may have been marked with far deeper wounds of rejection. But it's not about comparing our scars to see who hurt more or who's the greater victim. It's about realizing that the devil targeted "all" of us to some degree because of our God-given destiny.

WHY IT HURTS SO BAD

Rejection lingers. It haunts. It scars the soul like no other human emotion. But, why is this? Why does it hurt so much? Why can't we just shrug it off? Why can't we just power off the feelings like a smartphone and move on? Why does rejection replay in our minds every day or precisely at the moment we're about to charge towards something new? That's when we get cold feet and wonder if we're just setting ourselves up for rejection again. Well, before I attempt to answer that, let's unshell what rejection actually is.

Rejection is the feeling of not being liked, accepted, loved, valued or received. It is the condition of feeling unwanted or unappreciated. When we internalize these feelings they can spin a web of other toxic feelings, such as, worthlessness, insecurity, guilt, shame, loneliness, resentment and bitterness. And this might only be scratching the surface. Studies have shown that rejection is such a strong emotion that the body actually registers the sensation as if it were a physical pain.

When we're rejected, it can create a malfunction in our personalities that short-circuits our relationship with God and with others. It changes our perception of ourselves to the point that we begin to believe that we *deserved* to be rejected. We'll wrongly believe that God's promises belong to others, but not us. We'll wrongly base our worth on how well we perform or how much we accomplish. The result of this mindset is destructive to your relationships and disastrous to your dreams.

The reason why rejection hurts so badly is because we were created for acceptance and wired for social belonging. It's a basic human need. Whenever we are rejected, it denies us the satisfaction that comes with the most sacred and secure kind of peace—the peace of absolute acceptance. Rejection hurts because it makes us feel like outcasts, like we're less than human.

We can't rejection-proof our lives. We shouldn't tiptoe through life, afraid of being rejected and hurt. The splendor of possessing God's promises come through faith, which requires vulnerability and risk-taking. Trying to avoid rejection won't make your life any happier or healthier. In fact, it could make you feel worse and deeply disconnected from life's most enriching experiences and rewarding relationships.

Remember, rejection is redirection. Therefore, you must

search for God's purpose and discover where you actually belong.

KINGDOM OF MISFITS

If you've ever been rejected, you're in good company. Of Jesus, the gospel writer tells us, *"He came to His own, and His own did not receive Him"* (John 1:11). When Christians talk about becoming more like Jesus, we usually mean to become more loving, tolerant, compassionate, unselfish or spiritual. Rarely do we consider the possibility that becoming more like Christ means dealing with the same types of challenges He faced. We all want to reign with Him. None of us want to suffer with Him. We want to know Him in the power of His resurrection, but not in the fellowship of His suffering. And really, who can blame us? Nobody likes to hurt. Nobody wants to be rejected. And certainly Jesus doesn't ask us to self-inflict our lives as some type of religious mortification. But through hurts like rejection, we stumble into a realm of grace and fellowship with Christ that cannot be realized any other way.

In the Apostle Peter's first letter, he took some time to explain how Jesus was rejected, yet became the foundation of our faith. Quoting the prophet Isaiah, Peter uses a construction analogy to describe Jesus' rejection and subsequent redirection: *"The stone which the builders rejected has become the chief cornerstone"* (1 Peter 2:7). My humble commentary on this verse is that Jesus was a misfit, but became the perfect fit for our eternal salvation. The Jews, especially the Pharisees, couldn't fit Jesus into their religious box of rules. He didn't look the part. He didn't act the part. He didn't read from the same script of the Pharisees and abide by all their self-righteous code of ethics. They rejected Jesus because they couldn't control Him – because He was different, because He exposed their hypocrisy, because He wasn't "one of them." If you're ever rejected because of your belief system or confession of Christ, you're in good company. If you ever feel like a misfit in this world because you profess godliness and carry a torch of truth, you're in good company.

What the Jews didn't realize was that their rejection of Jesus would actually redirect Him towards His ultimate purpose—to die on a cross for our sins and raise Himself up three days later as the triumphant King. The rejected stone would become the chief cornerstone in God's great building called "the church."

From the moment Jesus was born, He was already a misfit. No one else on earth could claim to be the Son of God. His genealogy was literally out of this world. There wasn't a person on the planet that could really relate to Him. And to think... He chose this path. Thing is, Jesus didn't have to become a misfit. He didn't have to leave the comfort of heaven to dwell among sinful dust. But because He loved us so extravagantly, He lowered Himself in the form of a man, knowing all along that those He came to serve would crucify Him. The power of the gospel is that the Son of God became like the sons of men, so that the sons of men could become like the Son of God. In other words, He became like us (misfits) so we could become like Him.

Not only was Jesus a misfit, but He also drafted twelve mismatched men with no religious training or pedigree to serve as His associates. They were a band of badly flawed individuals who differed in social class, personality and background. They constantly battled their doubts and misunderstood what Jesus was trying to teach them. Yet, Jesus hand-selected these twelve disciples to eventually leave in charge after He returned to heaven. Clearly, Jesus saw something in these men that they didn't see in themselves. It takes a misfit to know a misfit.

After three and a half years of training, these disciples were commissioned with the job of spreading the gospel all over the world and leading the early church. They had learned a lot under Jesus, but as time went on, they still couldn't shake the misfit label off their lives. In Acts 4:13, after a physical miracle, the Sanhedrin called Peter and John's credentials into question: *"Now when they saw the boldness of Peter and John, and perceived that they were uneducated and untrained men, they marveled. And they realized that they had been with Jesus."* The only thing these men could do was "own it" and use it to prove their naysayers wrong. The Sanhedrin could label them misfits and reject their credentials, but they could not deny that "they had been with Jesus," nor could they refute the physical evidence of a lame man who was now walking as a normal man.

I don't believe God glories in my rejection, but that He uses my rejection for His glory. He doesn't take pleasure in my pain, but uses my pain for His purpose. He may not have caused my rejection, but He will use my rejection for His cause. If you're a misfit, you fit into the kingdom. And before you think about skipping this chapter, I am willing to bet that we all have felt like misfits, rejects or unqualified candidates in some aspect of our lives. Live your life long enough and someone or something will reject you.

Everyone experiences rejection. It's how you respond to it that will either prevent or propel you into your purpose.

GOD SELECTS WHAT MAN REJECTS

Whether you've got skin thinner than tissue paper or thicker than tree bark, rejection still cuts. You don't have to pretend it doesn't. You don't have to act like you're immune to the pain of rejection. That attitude won't help you one bit. Rejection is a feeling that we never get used to. So we might as well talk about it and figure out what we can learn from it, how we can grow from it, how we can use it to propel our lives forward instead of slipping backwards. In fact, let's conduct a little survey right now. Raise your hand if you have *never* heard any of the following lines in one form or another:

- Let's just be friends.
- It's not you; it's me.
- Unfortunately, we don't have a position that meets your qualifications at this time.
- We regret to inform you that we cannot grant you acceptance to X University.
- We're sorry you were not approved for this loan.
- You won't get the house you wanted.
- You didn't get enough votes.

- I love you son/daughter, but dad and mom can't live together anymore, so I'll be moving out.
- Regrettably, due to cutbacks and restructuring, the company has to lay you off.

Read this next sentence carefully. Whatever or whomever rejected you might have done you the biggest favor. Now, before you object, allow me to qualify that statement—because I know it doesn't feel that way and I know such a claim seems ludicrous. As I look over my life, there were certain moments of rejection that made me question my worth and doubt whether or not I would bounce back. I can sit here and act super spiritual, like I never waivered in my faith or complained about my disappointments, but that wouldn't be very honest or helpful. But I have come to realize that rejection prepares you for acceptance. In fact, you can't really grasp or understand how accepted you are until you've been rejected. You can't appreciate what you have, unless you've lost something. You can't fully appreciate your salvation until you recognize you were a sinner and deserved God's wrath. Maybe that sounds harsh, but those who usually return to a life of sin never understood how bad it was in the first place.

Rejection is not a positive experience, but it can produce a positive outcome. In my case, rejection pushed me into my calling to preach. Right after high school I made a decision to enroll into Bible College full-time. I needed to run towards the place where I felt like I belonged, where I could "be me" after years of trying to fit in. I don't know if I was technically ready for Bible College, either. But I couldn't imagine myself living through another phase of life where I suppressed who I really was. I could not dismiss my calling. I realized that what disqualified me from places I wanted to be, qualified me for places I needed to be. I realized that God doesn't call the qualified, but He qualifies the called. Our rejection awakens us to God's selection. Running towards God's love and calling gave me great assurance, not because I suddenly became perfect, but because I realized that Jesus had already accepted me at my worst, at my lowest, at my messiest. Since God called and accepted us at our worst, we owe Him our best.

Live *from* His acceptance, not *for* His acceptance. Stop trying to earn what's already been freely given to you.

Don't live *in fear* of God's rejection, but *in faith* through God's acceptance.

In Paul's first letter to the Corinthians, he addresses his concerns about sectarianism, which is basically when very similar religious groups divide over the finer points of their doctrines and beliefs, and then seek to have preeminence over each other. That's the best I can explain it. But it can actually get quite extreme and even violent in some regions of the world. Anyhow, Paul discerned that certain church members in Corinth had an elitist mentality and were acting snobby based on who baptized them or their religious pedigree.

In an effort to level the playing field and bring some perspective, Paul reminds us that God doesn't play favorites and that He often doesn't call those who are "great." It's actually the reverse. He calls the weak and rejected. Read Paul's words for yourself: *"For you see your calling, brethren, that not many wise according to the flesh, not many mighty, not many noble, are called. But God has chosen the foolish things of the world to put to shame the wise, and God has chosen the weak things of the world to put to shame the things which are mighty"* (1 Cor. 1:26-27). According to Paul, your brokenness and weakness doesn't disqualify you from God's use. On the contrary, it's why Jesus chose you. We often think of God choosing us *in spite of* our weaknesses. That's not the worst thing, either. In fact, it that was the whole truth, there would still be reason enough to be grateful to God. That would still make me feel assured and accepted. The fact that God would look beyond my faults and weaknesses is incredible. To use a pro sports draft analogy, even if I was chosen in the third or forth rounds, after all the top prospects were selected, I would probably still be thankful to be on the team.

But I've got better news than that.

You ready?

God didn't just choose you *in spite* of your weaknesses; He chose you *because of* your weaknesses.

Paul reveals why God does this: *"that no flesh should glory in His presence. But of Him you are in Christ Jesus, who became for us wisdom from God—and righteousness and sanctification and redemption—that, as it is written, "He who glories, let him glory in the Lord"* (1 Cor. 1:29-30). God looking *beyond* your flaws is both lovely and true, but the whole truth is that He selected you *based* on your flaws, so that He might glorify Himself through your life. God doesn't simply tolerate your weaknesses, but uses them to reveal His glory and grace. He doesn't simply tolerate your flaws; He flows through your flaws.

You can take your broken pieces and cut yourself or others. Or you can allow God to create a mosaic – a perfectly imperfect work of art. I believe the church is like a mosaic of stained glass windows, broken people pieced together to tell the story of God's grace, so that His light can shine through us. Beautifully broken.

God saw beauty in your mess because He saw the potential of glory. He longs to be glorified through our lives. He wants to shine through the cracks in our heart. The reasons that others rejected you are the very same reasons why Jesus chose you.

EJECT YOUR REJECTION

I wrote this book to help you move forward in God's hope and through the power of God's Spirit. What the devil means for evil, God turns it around for the good of His purpose. You are not helpless. It's time to take back your destiny. So at this point, I would like to provide you with three actions to eject rejection from your life and/or minimize its impact.

1. Accept God's Acceptance

As a victim of rejection, the worst thing you can probably do is reject acceptance. The only way to break free from the death-grip of rejection is to know your true self-worth, to know acceptance from the One who had every reason to reject you — but He didn't. The miracle of God's acceptance is that He selected us in our worst and most broken state. Living *from*

God's acceptance, when we deserved rejection, should sooth the minor rejections we experience from day to day. It should also alleviate the pressures to always be perfect and compare your progress with other people.

According to John, *"We love Him because He first loved us"* (1 John 4:19). We can accept God freely, because He accepted us first. The pain of rejection is dissolved in the presence of your loving Father, who against all logic, wrapped your soul in His warm and safe arms. If you haven't already, I urge you, throw yourself into the soft but sturdy arms of Jesus, who will go before you and never abandon you. Jesus is faithful.

Accept His acceptance. Don't run from the one place where you are loved on the basis of your weaknesses and brokenness. Don't hide from the One whose love will carry you in times of despair and restlessness, the One who smiles over the thought of you, the One who will never cast you out, the One who became your rejection on the cross and defeated it when the stone rolled away.

2. Forgive your Rejecters

The process of ejecting rejection from your life will never complete until you forgive those who hurt you. Forgiving your rejecters requires an understanding of God's fierce forgiveness in your own life. Paul wrote, *"...as Christ forgave you, so you also must do"* (Colossians 3:13). It can be very difficult (for some, impossible) to arrive at a place of forgiving someone who offended or wounded you. It's not something we naturally do. Our natural reaction is to retaliate or hold a grudge.

When you forgive someone who rejected you, specifically, forgiving him or her may feel like you're *accepting their rejection*, like you're allowing them to reject you—over and over. Be assured, forgiving is not accepting their motive for rejection; it's dismissing the ongoing pain of rejection that can keep you going in circles.

Don't get stuck in your feelings of rejection by refusing to forgive. Your life is too important. Your purpose is too significant. The devil wants to keep you bound and caged in resentment over who rejected you. But greater is He that is in you. The Holy Spirit will give you the grace to forgive and let go. When you do, you will be set free to live deeper and love deeper.

3. Guard your Heart

The Bible says, *"Keep your heart with all diligence, for out of it spring the issues of life"* (Proverbs 4:23). I think it's vitally important to emphasize how you can minimize the sting of rejection. We must also learn not to take certain rejections so personally, so deeply, by simply keeping a realistic outlook. Some of the rejection feelings people have are due to over-idealizing some career or relationship in the future. They overinvest into ideals that most likely will not transpire in the real world—like expecting a perfect spouse, perfect kids, perfect church, perfect friendships and a perfect job. I'm not saying you should just settle for less. But guard your heart from the things that have the tendency to veer into fantasyland. Perfect spouses and kids don't exist. Neither does perfect churches and perfect ministry leaders. The dream job you're applying for—guess what—that's not perfect either because you'll be working with imperfect people.

You can't let others' reactions and acceptance become the driving forces in your life. Don't empower people to decide your general mood and approach to life. Don't over-depend on others to affirm you. Be driven by your convictions and your callings—whether they are warmly accepted or coldly criticized. You'll be happier once you accept that you can't make everyone happy.

You'll also need to learn the difference between the rejection of your idea and the rejection of "you." People may reject my idea or disagree with my decision, but that doesn't mean they have rejected *me*. If you confuse the two, it could lead to mistaken hurt feelings and a false sense of rejection.

You can't move on into your destiny until you get over the hurt feelings of rejection, until you allow God's acceptance to define your value and shape your world. If rejection hasn't been a big issue for you, perhaps the issue I discuss in the next chapter—failure—has kept you stuck in pain and from moving forward.

{Chapter 8}

Breaking your Silence

I am a private person. Which makes this book a little tougher than previous books I've written. Parts of this book have been very personal. I've shared intimate details about my life that I don't frequently talk about. As an author, I have always tried to limit or avoid this. It's a big risk. *What if my story is misinterpreted?* Or worse, *what if I'm viewed differently or judged negatively?* Once something is published, there's no getting it back. That is why the chapter you are reading now was never supposed to be written. I wish I didn't have to. Honestly, I fought it. At times, I refused and shuttered at the thought.

This chapter is about thirty years in the making.

That's right. Thirty years.

Because for the first time, I am going to publicly share one of my darkest secrets—one that up until a few years ago had remained locked and sealed away in the deepest chamber of my heart. After years and years of silence, I am finally opening up in order to help those who have experienced similar pain or feel shackled by a dark secret of any nature. I'm breaking my silence to help you break yours, to help you heal and find hope again.

My painful secret is that as a boy, I was sexually molested. I would like to tell you my story and how my process of inner healing began.

WHEN THE ICE THAWED

The events in my life thirty years ago were frozen in time. The memory has always been there — encased in a thick block of ice with all the details perfectly preserved in my mind. For years I could see it, but couldn't feel it. I didn't know how to feel about it. My memory, although intact, came with little emotion other than disbelief. I went through long stretches of time without ever thinking about it—which is why I didn't consider it a "problem" for me. Year after year, my mind would coat the memory with fresh layers of ice. In my gut, I didn't want to believe I was a victim. So, I convinced myself that I wasn't. Life would be simpler that way. Less complicated. Less messy. And, plus, I didn't have the energy or desire to hammer through those thick layers. I was enjoying my life.

Years had gone by. I was doing fine. I graduated from High School. I went to Bible college. I got ordained into ministry. I married the girl of my dreams. *Why make a big deal about some-*

thing that hasn't affected me, held me back or damaged my life? I'm not wounded. I'm not a victim. Just shovel some snow on that block of ice and move on. Life is good. Don't mess it up.

Facing the reality of past sexual abuse is a process. It does not happen overnight or in one climatic moment of transparency. The first person I told was my wife. It was either right before we were married or right after. I honestly can't remember when I told her. And I think it's because it wasn't emotionally that climatic of a moment. The block was still frozen solid. I talked about it with zero emotion because as married couples do, we shared everything about our lives. I didn't want to keep any secrets from her. So, it was more informative, not therapeutic. I figured, *the woman I'm going to spend the rest of my life with should know my past.*

I suppose there were moments that had the potential to crack the ice of this memory, such as hearing others open up about their sexual abuse. It made me ponder my experience. But I was committed to my story—*I'm not a victim. I'm not wounded.*

Case closed.

So I thought.

As I entered my 30's, life started to change. I was now a dad. My son, Makai, caused me to see the world in a different way. Now that I was the provider and protector for this innocent, defenseless child, the world became a little darker. My protective instincts kicked in. News stories about neighborhood crimes, car accidents and child endangerment that used to pass through my ears, now troubled me. All of the sudden, the world didn't feel so safe. I was being forced to think about injustice in ways that I had never bothered to.

Slowly, the ice around my sexual abuse began to melt without me realizing it. Drip by drip. Year by year.

When my daughter, Chloe, was born, it was like pointing a hair dryer directly on the ice at max heat. A puddle had formed under the block. Flashbacks of what was done to me were lingering longer than normal. The memory was getting a little messier to manage, but again, I had a story to keep—one that I had believed for too long. *These are just minor flashbacks, speedbumps in my heart,* I reasoned. *Get a grip, Jacob. You're too old for this. Maybe you're a victim, maybe you're not, but it doesn't matter anymore. Crank up the cold and man up. Your kids are counting on you to be strong. You're a pastor and a national youth leader, too. You don't need this right now. Snap out of it.*

I was rough on myself. I didn't advise myself the way I would advise someone else, which made me feel worse.

The devil also knows my past. I could hear voices of fear and doubt shuttering through my mind – voices saying, *"Don't talk about this. You're acting weak. No one needs to know. People will think less of you. You've got an image to uphold. Keep silent".*

But in 2016, the ice block thawed. The thick layers that once separated me from the incident had dissolved, making my soul feel naked and vulnerable. I couldn't distance myself from the hurt anymore. I was feeling emotions that I had never felt. I was asking questions that I had never asked.

There was the memory, after the ice completely melted away. Frame by frame. The scene of my injustice had been perfectly preserved like a 3D model. Not only could I remember how everything looked, but I could practically feel the humidity in that garage and touch the dust on the old smelly furniture. I can still sense my eyes adjusting as I'm lured into the dark, dingy spaces behind all the clutter and away from view. Preserved in its original state, I can paint a picture of even the most mundane details. I cannot go into the specifics of what happened. Not only is it too painful, but I don't want to glorify the abuse or the abuser. Victims of sexual abuse will know where I'm coming from.

What I couldn't figure out is, why now?

Why after all these years, am I feeling this way?

Then one day it dawned on me. I connected some dots in my mind and realized what was happening. My son, Makai, had just turned the age I was when these acts were committed against me. Seeing him was like looking at myself at that age. It triggered something. And I could no longer hide from the hard, cold parts of my soul that were thawing with every hug and moment spent with my amazing son. The polar ice cap of secret pain and injustice had melted in the warmth of my son's innocence. His sweet kisses on my prickly cheeks and tight hugs around my legs helped me face a reality that I spent decades avoiding.

At this point, I also realized that God had changed the climate around my soul in order to set me free at last from the shame, the denial, the mislabeling, the minimizing that had kept my heart frozen.

I couldn't keep silent anymore. But every time I worked up some courage to talk about it, fear would flood my mind. I would reason within myself: *your wife knows, that's enough.* But I knew that wasn't enough. I needed to tell two of the most important people in my life, whose hearts would be crushed to powder—my mom and dad. I didn't want to hurt them, see them cry, and have them second-guess any decisions they made as parents. I know and believe that nothing they could have done would have prevented this from happening. There was no way of knowing that the kid who did this to me was even capable of such things. I was preyed on; plain and simple. I don't blame my parents and didn't want them to blame themselves.

I wrestled with my fears for months.

Should I say something? Should I not?

I battled back and forth.

Suppressing my pain felt like trying to hold a beach ball underwater. Only, this ball kept growing. I couldn't keep it under anymore. Finally, I decided to open up. I couldn't take it anymore. I was tired of hiding from the truth. So, I got my phone and texted my parents, *"We need to talk."* And the next morning, we did.

It was one of the most difficult conversations I've ever had. When I sat down, my lips tightened up, and my eyelids held back tears like the Hoover Dam. After a few minutes of setting up my story, I finally admitted: *"When I was a boy, I was sexually molested."*

The dam broke.

And so did my chains.

I'm a grown man but I sobbed in my parents' arms like a child. I cried for the eight-year-old boy in me who had been muzzled in fear and shame for too long – the boy who had his sexuality victimized and stolen. Those tears were painful, but hopeful. As I bared my soul, I could feel the love of God beginning to heal my life. I am grateful for my wife, my parents and family for their love and support. I don't know what I would do without them.

I've since changed my story. *I was a victim. What was done to me was wrong and should have never happened. By His stripes, I am healed and free from the shackles of shame and fear. I am not "my abuse," I am a child of God.*

That is my new story. But the script is still being written through a process of naming the pain, undoing the denial, wrestling with questions, and understanding the role and work of the Holy Spirit to bring change and healing.

OUT OF HIDING

Part of what kept my memory frozen for so long, was that I was both unwilling and afraid to face the reality of what happened to me. You cannot conquer what you're unwilling to confront. No matter what pain you're hiding from the past, you must break your silence in order to be healed. Your past wounds might be different than mine. In my case, it was sexual abuse. But whatever your wound is, you will not find total freedom and healing until you unlock that dark secret, until the skeletons in the closet are revealed. What you hide, hides you – masking the person you were created to be.

Thanks to Adam and Eve who sinned and, because of fear and shame, hid from the presence of God, it's human nature to mask our pain and disguise our issues. We pretend that everything is fine, when we're really hurting inside. James 5:16 tells us, *"Confess your faults one to another, and pray one for another, that ye may be healed. The effectual fervent prayer of a righteous man availeth much."* I have found that this verse not only applies to our faults, but our wounds.

Not only did I battle hard with accepting what happened to me, but I battled to say it. Once you say something, it brings a memory, an experience into reality. It is no longer a nebulous recollection or emotion. I didn't want to label this truth. Because as long as it didn't have a label, it wasn't "real." But until you label your pain, you're just shadow boxing—swinging at the wind and draining your energy.

A couple of years ago, I was having a conversation with two friends of mine, when slowly the topic veered towards the issues of sexual abuse. I don't even remember how the topic came up. But I couldn't believe how openly both men talked about their abuse and how they had coped. Until then, I had no idea they were victims. I would have never guessed it. But their openness made me nervous. I could feel my heart pumping blood inside my chest and my palms beginning to sweat. I stood there silent and motionless like a scarecrow, but inside I was screaming, *"me too!"*

I remember driving home that night feeling so trapped in reluctance. I was scared to define my experience. But the ice had thawed and it was time to face reality. I only wish I had faced it sooner. Only God knows.

After Adam sinned, he sewed fig leaves together to cover up his shame. We have a tendency to cover those areas of life that cause shame, hurt or frustration. The dilemma is not necessarily that we don't want others, or God, to see our issues. It is that we ourselves don't want to see, deal with, or confront the wounds of the past. This is how I felt about my past. I didn't want to admit or address the dark parts about my life. It's much easier to mask it with religion, money, humor, or friends, than to peel back the Band-Aid on my unhealed pain.

That's why God asked Adam, *"Where are you?"* God didn't ask for Himself, but for Adam. It was that Adam needed to face his own failures and wounds. He needed to recognize his own need for restoration. He needed to come to terms with his condition and face his fears.

I struggled to admit my abuse because I didn't want to make a mess. I didn't want to be a burden on anybody. I didn't want to open a can of worms. But the can of worms from the past that you don't open will only multiply over time, until it's a tank of worms.

The reason we shut the door on our pain is because it's more convenient. Like closing the door to a messy room in your house, you can walk around, have dinner parties, clean other rooms, and not feel pressured by the messy room.

Why? The door is closed.

But no matter how much you sweep the kitchen floor and wipe the bathroom sink, *the house* is still out of order because of that one messy room. While closing the door eases your conscience, it doesn't change the reality that things are not as they should be.

Maybe you're thinking, *Wait a minute! God loves me. You mean to say that God won't heal me unless I reveal the issue?* Exactly. Remember, Jesus is a perfect gentleman who stands at the door and knocks. He won't come in unless invited.

We deny our pain. We pretend it really doesn't matter. We close the door. But all we are really doing is living in denial. All the while, God wants to heal, restore and lift the burden off your life. Yet, we make it classified information. Not only because we're afraid of others knowing. But because we know that if it's exposed, we have to face off with our fears.

It's time to remove your mask and expose your true need. The only way God can deliver you is for you to bare your scariest secrets and thoughts. You must let go of your grip. It's time to open up to someone you really trust and free yourself from the web of shame and fear. Quit punishing yourself for things that God has already forgiven you of. Stop agonizing about your past and things you had no control over. No more overcompensating in other areas of life to balance out the guilt or shame you carry.

Your mask isn't just affecting you. It could affect your family and especially your children. Your disguise can become their disguise. Your kids don't just have your eyes or your hair color; they adopt your habits. They are learning from you. Be healed so your family can stay healed.

We all struggle. We all have scars. Nobody's life is perfect. We're human. But if Jesus is ever going to do a miracle in your life, you have to acknowledge and expose the issue for what it is. When a child falls, and injures himself or herself, the first thing a parent will say is, *"Show me where it hurts."* Because unless the area of pain is revealed, you can't properly apply the solution. God is saying, *"Show me where it hurts. If you reveal it; I will heal it."*

You don't have to go to bed another night, feeling oppressed or enslaved to your hidden issues. Come out from where you are. Come out from under the blankets of regret and shame. Come out from the cave of isolation. Dust yourself off. Rinse out your grudges and despair. You are not *what* you went through. Your infirmity is not your identity. You were a victim, but you're not a victim. You made a mistake, but you're not a mistake. You might feel lonely, but you're not alone. Just because you have gone through a terrible time of affliction, your heavenly Father still sees the value within your soul. You are a child of God.

Believe that with all your heart.

KEYS TO INNER HEALING

Before I continue in this section, I have a small disclaimer. I am a pastor with a college degree in Theology, but I am not a licensed therapist or professional counselor. If you feel you need professional help, which many do, you should seek it. There is no shame in that. I fear that too many Christians live with secret wounds because they're ashamed or feel unspiritual for seeking guidance in the form of Christian counseling. Nothing could be further from the truth. We need to swallow our religious pride and get the help we need when or if we need it. I want to be transparent about my credentials and my intentions.

That being said, I still believe my advice is worth following because my story is worth telling, and I survived to tell it. It's always a good idea to learn from those who slayed the giants your fighting.

KEY 1 – TELL YOURSELF THE TRUTH

The first key to breaking your silence and beginning the process of inner healing is to *start telling yourself the truth.*

For thirty years, I sculpted an ice block of denial around my victimhood. I had thoroughly convinced myself that the incidents were merely a memory malfunction, or at least a misinterpretation of events. It was easier to create my own version of history—a safer, more palatable version that insolated my mind from places too dark to tread. I choose to believe a lie, a storyline that allowed me to sleep at night. Maybe it was a subconscious effort to protect myself. Whatever it was, it worked for a very long time. But the truth is stubborn. It refuses to go away. It doesn't take "no" for an answer. It gnawed away at me until I finally made the decision that I would rather deal with the pain of breaking my silence, then the pain of keeping it.

Your past will haunt your present until you confront it. The older you get, and the more life settles down, the harder it will be to hide from the past. Some people have determined to suppress their secrets and will sadly take them to the grave. But hear me, please. That is not the will of God for your life. That is not how your story should end. The truth must come out. It screams for attention. It demands a verdict, even if only an emotional one. Jesus said, *"You shall know the truth, and the truth shall make you free"* (John 8:32). We avoid the truth because sometimes the truth hurts. It will hurt you and it might hurt others, too. But it's the only way to be free.

Your inner healing will start when you get totally honest with yourself and identify the source of your pain. Restoration cannot begin until you fully face the problem. You must collide with the raw, deep-tissue truth in order to heal and receive what only Jesus can offer.

And there is something powerful about verbally admitting the truth. When I spoke the truth aloud in front of my parents, it not only validated my pain, but it helped define the allusive emotions that were starting to control my mind. Admitting the truth broke a levee of lies and gave way to a gush of freedom that I'd been thirsting for.

Truth exposes your thirst. When you speak it, or hear it, you discover dry places you've been trying to quench without even realizing it. When you finally recognize and speak the truth of your pain and of God's Word, the mercies of heaven will sweep over your soul like the Jordan River—leaving your cup spilling over. You don't need a cup when you're in the river. Just drink and be refreshed.

KEY 2 – LET GO OF SHAME

After telling yourself the truth, the second key to inner healing is to *let go of shame.* Part of what kept me silent for so long was a cloak of shame around my heart. Yes, I was embarrassed. But it cut deeper than that. I was ashamed of myself. Maybe you're thinking, *"Why were you ashamed? You were the victim".* Believe me; I told myself this over and over. But in my silence, I couldn't shake off the feeling of shame. The more aware I became of my shame, the worse I felt. I was ashamed of being *ashamed.* I started to feel responsible for my sexual abuse. For years, I rationalized: *It's my fault too. I must have done something to entice the abuser. I let it happen. Why didn't I say anything earlier?*

Shame takes on different forms. Yours could be related to something you regret doing or not doing. Shame could stem not only from the incident itself, but from how you coped with it and who you might have hurt in the process. Hurt people *hurt* people—which only adds to the shame you already feel.

Adam's recognition of shame came as a direct result of eating of the tree of the knowledge of good and evil. Before that moment of disobedience, the Bible says that Adam and Eve *"were not ashamed"* (Ref. Genesis 2:25). Now, thousands of years later the same cycle of hiding shameful emotions is repeating itself in believers and unbelievers alike. It's time to break that ancient cycle. What many people may not realize is that shame is the root of many other toxic emotions, including hatred, arrogance, fear, blame, and self-absorption. It can lead to broken relationships, intimacy issues, and isolation. Shame won't allow you to be vulnerable enough to develop healthy and trusting friendships. It could keep you from feeling fully connected with God and others.

Shame wants to hide. It confuses silence with solace – secrecy with privacy. It doesn't want you to see how it's influencing your emotions, behaviors and decisions. It distorts the truth about your pain and dismantles your self-worth. It's no wonder why the devil works around the clock to keep people shackled in a cycle of shame.

But I have good news; a healthy heart is right around the corner. Jesus came to set you free from shame and take your captivity captive.

The Gospel is the antidote to shame. We need to understand that Jesus took our shame and nailed it to the cross. Listen to the prophet Isaiah portray the sufferings of Jesus as the cure to our deepest needs—salvation and restoration: *"Surely He has borne our griefs and carried our sorrows; Yet we esteemed Him stricken, Smitten by God, and afflicted. But He was wounded for our transgressions, He was bruised for our iniquities; The chastisement for our peace was upon Him, and by His stripes we are healed"* (Isaiah 53:4-5). The word "sorrows" in this passage, literally translates as grief, pain, or affliction. When Jesus shed His blood, He carried away our inner wounds. He lifted the emotional baggage off our shoulders. The Word of God tells us that He cares for us, and we can cast all of our cares upon Him (Ref. 1 Peter 5:7).

Release your shame into the hands of God.

The devil tried to utterly destroy you.

But he failed miserably. Satan's plot failed before it ever hatched, because the plan of God is greater. What the enemy meant for evil, God turned around for your good.

KEY 3 – PRAY AND READ GOD'S WORD

The third key is to *spend time in prayer and in God's Word.* God invites you into His presence and will transform you by renewing your mind (Ref. Romans 12:2). You must carve out quality time for prayer and study of God's Word. Prayer isn't about "mind over matter," clearing mental clutter, or becoming more self-aware in order to heal oneself. This is a secular humanistic view that millions of people spend millions of dollars trying to achieve. It's a widely embraced and integrated belief system in society and its chief end is the deification of man. It's "Me-ism." That's not what I'm promoting in this book or this chapter. Self-meditation is not prayer. Prayer is not a dialogue with yourself. Prayer is a dialogue with God. And I am sold on the idea that without prayer, we cannot transform or restore our lives according to the purpose of God. Speaking from my own experience, I honestly don't know how I would have survived my pain and found inner healing without a prayer life.

In prayer, the Holy Spirit ministered to me and conducted spiritual open-heart surgery. I know it sounds so simple, so plain, but prayer works. I believe in the power of prayer and the effects it has on the soul and spirit. Prayer was the place where I really confronted my past and cried out to God with cries too piercing for human ears. Prayer is where I abandoned my false theories, accepted the reality of my sexual victimhood and found comfort in the arms of Jesus. Maybe it sounds like I'm overselling prayer. Maybe you're wondering, *can prayer really help me like that?*

Many Christians dislike how generic, basic and time-consuming it sounds when someone says, *"just pray more,"* because we all know we're supposed to pray anyways. But the truth is, there isn't a remedy on the planet that can substitute the necessity and power of prayer. It's just that our flesh, our wounded spirit, would rather pop a pill, hear a sermon, take an action, do something (anything) but kneel down and make ourselves pray to God. In other words, we just want results and we want them *now.* We want the pain to go away. Who can blame us for that? We want relief from the hurt. But inner healing is a process that is facilitated by daily doses of prayer and the Word.

Prayer is the secret place and the place of secrets. It is a spiritual garden where you can be yourself, where your soul can be naked and unashamed before your Creator. The devil will fight you over your prayer time. He will attack your prayer life from every angle with distractions, busyness, boredom and tiredness—anything to keep you unplugged from heaven's power grid.

Then when you mix the Word of God into your prayer, something even more powerful happens. Over the years, I've developed the habit of praying the Word of God. It's reading passages as if they were my own words. Inner healing will come as you pray healing scriptures. The psalmist wrote, *"He sent His word and healed them, and delivered them from their destructions"* (Psalm 107:20). Pray with your Bible open and let the Word of

Life inscribe and prescribe what you need to heal from your wounds.

KEY 4 – FORGIVE YOUR OFFENDER

You probably saw this one coming. But the fourth and final key I'll mention is to *forgive your offender*. Forgiving my abuser was hard. Only through applying the keys I've mentioned, and a sheer awakening of God's grace in my own life, was I able to forgive. I've touched on the issue of forgiveness throughout this book and I could simply fire off a list of scriptures about forgiveness and say, *"Forgive because Jesus said to. That settles it"*. But I realize that it's a real struggle to forgive, even when we know we ought to.

I'm going to be real with you. Sometimes our efforts to forgive only deepen our wounds or self-inflict with shame when we can't properly obey Christ's command. We want to be good Bible-believing Christians and follow simple orders, but life can be very complicated. I think many people are living with broken views of forgiveness that lead to rushed resolutions and duct-tape repairs on relationships that really need to be rebuilt. We tend to force wounded or offended people into quick religious fixes that don't really heal the heart from bitterness. We're so afraid to feel negative emotions that we patch up our problems in order to appear like everything is fine—when really, we're just going through the motions. I've been guilty of doing that. News flash: it doesn't work.

We quote Jesus praying on the cross, *"Father, forgive them for they don't know what they do"* to persuade people to forgive, without deeply considering His other haunting prayer, *"My God,*

My God, why have you forsaken me?" Jesus forgave His crucifiers, but also appeared to have serious doubts and relational pain with His Father. This is just an example of how jumbled our human emotions can get and how complex the process of healing can be. We forgive people, but then panic sets in when we still feel pain and sadness over what happened to us—which causes us to question the legitimacy of our forgiveness. *If I forgave him, why am I still hurting? Why does the memory still bring tears to my eyes? If I forgave her, why am I still angry?*

Forgiveness is not denying or excusing the hurt caused by abuse or offense. Too often, victims feel powerless to forgive because they've accepted wrong definitions of what it means to forgive. There are some myths on forgiveness that I would like to expose that may change your life. The first myth is that *forgiving someone removes the pain they caused.* Forgiving doesn't erase the memory and pain. You must understand the difference between forgiving and forgetting, between forgiving and healing. Just because you forgave someone, doesn't mean you're healed from the pain they caused. When I first broke my silence about my sexual abuse, I had already forgiven the abuser in my heart. But that didn't mean the pain was gone. In fact, the pain got worse, because I was hurting and couldn't blame anyone—which was a form of coping. A wound isn't going to heal overnight because you stated your forgiveness. But in time, the hemorrhage in your soul will stop and a scar will form in your memory like scars form over wounds of the body.

The second myth is that *forgiving someone excuses the damage they did.* People wrongly believe that to forgive someone means that you condone what they did, essentially saying what happened to you was okay. This is not the case. You don't sweep the abuse or the offense under the rug and pretend it was okay. Instead, you fully acknowledge that your pain is real and your abuser was wrong, but are willing to revoke revenge (Ref. Romans 12:17). When you forgive, you surrender your right to hurt someone for hurting you. The third myth is that *forgiving someone is a feeling*. We forgive because God forgave us. And His forgiveness was a choice, not a feeling. I doubt Jesus felt like forgiving those who crucified Him. I doubt He was in the mood. Jesus forgave because He decided to. Some hold back forgiveness because they're waiting for a certain feeling to come. That feeling might not ever come. But we are still called to follow the example of Christ and forgive, regardless of how it makes us feel.

If you believe you should forgive, then you will forgive on your timetable, when you're ready. I will circle back later to the issues of bitterness and forgiveness as it relates to healing relationships—which is a different process altogether. But for the moment, I ask that you take the keys of inner healing in your hands. Whether or not you're "ready" to break your silence and embark on a journey towards healing, is entirely up to you. I mean that in the most caring way. I didn't write this chapter to pressure you into admitting something you're not ready to admit, to confess something you're not sure about. I know how hard it is to open up about your pain. It might take every ounce of courage you have. But God will help you. You're not alone. Whatever you do, don't run from it. Don't hold yourself hostage in denial. Don't wait thirty years like I did.

The shame that has tried to keep you in silent agony, the fear that has kept your voice in a soundproof room, the loneliness that made you feel like driftwood in the sea – all of it – will slowly evaporate as you speak the truth and soak in the presence of God. Your road to inner healing will begin when you break your silence.

{Chapter 9}

Failing Forward

Before we launched CityLight Church in the fall of 2013, I endured a season where I struggled to see how God was going to bless my life again and re-open doors for my ministry. The reason? My past attempt to build a better life and ministry in Southern California had tanked. I felt like everything we worked for had short-circuited. As I've stated before, my plan was *not* to leave Southern California, especially not after only two years. My plan was to stay there. That's why we bought a home and didn't rent. That's why we started our family there. We planted roots. We established ourselves. I embraced the Inland Empire, with all its gridlock traffic, air pollution and dry Santa Ana winds. It became home. And I was happy. I once thought to myself, *if I should ever pastor a church, it would be here.* I didn't have a backup plan. No Plan B. I never imagined that in two quick years, I would be loading up the moving truck again and making the long, humbling drive back to the Bay Area.

I tried hard to keep a positive outlook and never really talked openly about how I felt. In fact, I confess that I even sugarcoated the story a little to sound more spiritual, as if God showed me a greater vision for my life and ministry. Have you ever tried that little maneuver? Be honest. It's that moment in a conversation when you're explaining to someone why things didn't go according to plan or how it completely bombed—but you don't want to sound like a loser, so you embellish some details or over-spiritualize to save face. Okay, maybe you've never done that. If so, I seriously admire you for it. I wasn't that brave. But I bet some reader is nodding their head and thinking, *yes, I'm guilty of the same.* Don't worry; your secret is safe with me.

The truth was, I had no idea what was going on and had no master plan. And one word kept slipping into my mind no matter how hard I tried to lock it out. One word kept flying around my head like a pesky housefly. That word was *failure*. I don't remember ever saying that word out loud to describe myself. But "failure" was packed away somewhere in the moving truck, and eventually I would have to face that baggage. At some point I had to confront my perceived failure and figure out a way to get over it. Because you can't embrace what is, if you're still holding onto what was. You can't stay stuck in feelings of failure and miss your purpose.

Failure is not the end of the world.

But again, let's be honest. Doesn't it feel that way sometimes? When you fail, hope dims and flickers in the winds of heartbreak. Whenever I fail, I take it personal. It usually takes some time to recover and collect my scattered thoughts, to treat my bruised ego. Nobody wants to be labeled a "failure." Nobody wants that stigma attached to his or her life. I've crossed paths with many people who live with regret over a past failure. They struggle to start over. They battle fears of failing again. They're stuck in the past, still nursing their wounds, and still replaying their failures in their minds—in slow motion.

What keeps us frozen in failure? Why does it affect us so deeply? It seems that failure from our past has a way of defining our identity and placing its limits on our calling. It seems we have a tendency to fixate on our faults and failures, which then distorts our perception of ourselves. Past failures roar at our dreams with intimidation. Let me be clear: this isn't God's will for your life. He called you for something greater. His promises for you and your family outweigh the regret of failure.

If you have been spiritually staggered because of failure, the time has come to awaken to your destiny in Christ and forget the past.

REMOVING THE "U" FROM FAILURE

Do you think of yourself as a failure in any area of your life? Many years ago I heard a leadership expert named Zig Ziglar define failure in a way that really put it into perspective. According to Ziglar, *"failure is an event, not a person."*

For years, this simple maxim has helped me to interpret my own failures and the failures of others. Because what so many of us do is internalize our failures and allow them to define our self-perception. The darkness of failure in one area of life tends to cloud other areas of life—to the point that you feel like a *total* failure. When my career failed in Southern California, it affected how I estimated my self-worth. I remember feeling like I had failed my wife and let down my son. I felt like less of a man. The reality was, I didn't do anything to fail my family. My marriage was healthy and our family unit was strong. But I had to step back and remember that failure is an event. I had to say to myself "I am not a failure."

Failure is one of those life events that can really get blown out of proportion and tends to become a lens that we look through—distorting everything we see. To curb that tendency and avoid those negative thinking patterns, you have to look at failure differently. You must isolate that failure to a specific moment or series of events and analyze it without attaching your worth to it. I know it's easier said than done. But you must remove the "u" from failure in order to learn from it. Now, let me clarify something. I'm not suggesting you run from responsibility or deny the part you played. Especially if you sinned, you need to repent, get right with God and those you may have hurt. Period. The issue of concern is when we allow failure to permanently stamp our lives. The issue is when we stay stuck in the past and allow failure to dictate how we live.

Let this sink in, *you are **not** your failure*. Maybe you failed. Maybe you made a mistake and regret what you did. And maybe there's no going back to fix it. We're not pretending we can change the past or denying its existence, but we can change today. You don't have to live the rest of your life under a curse of shame and a cloud of regret. You must filter every failure and mistake through the Word of God—His grace and atoning sacrifice for your sins. In other words, your failure is under the blood! It can't hold you unless you let it. It can't define unless you allow it.

Your sins are forgiven and forgotten.

The thick crust of your past is broken off your life and your failure is not final. You must believe it and confess it over your life, in Jesus Name. Your calling is too great to get stuck in failure and disappointment. But if you do feel stuck or like you can't remove the "u" in failure, I want you to know that it's not uncommon to feel that way. In fact, there are many examples from the Bible of people who struggled to remove the "u" in their failures and carried their past into their futures. One in particular was a woman named Naomi. Her failure was a broken dream for her family, a gamble for a better life that backfired.

DON'T CHANGE YOUR NAME

After her dreams crumbled and her husband and two sons died in Moab, Naomi and her daughter-in-law Ruth returned home to Bethlehem. As old friends greeted her, it triggered a reaction in Naomi that revealed how hurt and disappointed she was. Specifically, it was hearing her name called that troubled her.

"Naomi, is that you?"

"Hey, Naomi. We miss you!"

"Naomi, Naomi!"

The name Naomi means "joy or pleasant." But that was certainly not how she felt. Her heart was filled with anything but that. Her soul was sour. She didn't feel like her name suggested. After burying her husband and two sons, and watching her dreams shatter, her name didn't fit her life. Years before, her family had moved to Moab to escape poverty and build a better life. They thought the grass was greener on the other side. But it turned out to be an epic mistake to leave Bethlehem in the land of Judah for the pagan territory of Moab. They got desperate and gambled their future. Then tragically, it all blew up in their faces. Now, Naomi is back home and trying to restart her life with her daughter-in-law tagging along, and she is in no mood to be called "Joy."

Can you blame her?

Hearing her name felt like salt on the wound, even though these old friends meant no offense. But when you're bitter, compliments can sound sarcastic; gestures can seem artificial; people can seem rude—even when they're not. In other words, bitterness distorts how you view yourself and those around you.

Naomi couldn't stand hearing her name anymore. It reminded her of what could have been and should have been, but wasn't. So she said, *"Do not call me Naomi; call me Mara, for the Almighty has dealt very bitterly with me. I went out full, and the Lord has brought me home again empty. Why do you call me Naomi, since the Lord has testified against me, and the Almighty has afflicted me?" (Ruth 1:20-21).*

Naomi's solution was to change her name to something that characterized how she felt on the inside. The name Mara means "bitter." Because of her failures, she was bitter with life and hearing her real name sounded like nails scratching against a chalkboard. She didn't want to hear it. But here's my advice to you. Don't let failure change your name. Don't let bitter feelings change your identity and your destiny in life. Once again, you are not your failure. The Word of God declares that your failure is not your fate, but your fertilizer. Look at what the Scriptures declare.

- *"For a righteous man may fall seven times and rise again, but the wicked shall fall by calamity"* (Proverbs 24:16).
- *"The steps of a good man are ordered by the Lord, and He delights in his way. Though he falls, he shall not be utterly cast down; For the Lord upholds him with His hand"* (Psalm 37:23-24).
- *"The Lord upholds all who fall, and raises up all who are bowed down"* (Psalm 145:14).
- *"Brethren, I do not count myself to have apprehended; but one thing I do, forgetting those things which are behind and reaching forward to those things which are ahead"* (Philippians 3:13).

Don't change your name. Instead, confess the Word of God in your life and use your failure to fuel your progress. The devil wants to sabotage your identity and slap a permanent label of failure on your back. But here's what you need to know, God hasn't changed His mind about you or subtracted any of His precious promises. God hasn't changed your name. He hasn't forsaken you. He hasn't forgotten you. In fact, you are still who God says you are. Your story isn't over. The most significant moment in Naomi's story might easily be overlooked, but contains a powerful insight about how God responds to our false attempts to change our names. Ruth 1:22 starts by saying,

"So Naomi returned…" Despite her attempts to be called "Mara," God refused to allow that bitter name to define her life. Heaven's name registry did not accept "Mara" as a new name. In the eyes of God, Naomi was still Naomi.

No matter how badly you messed up, you are still who God says you are and you can become who He's calling you to be. I would like for you to consider some positive affects of failure and what it can reveal about your life.

LEARNING FROM FAILURE

If you don't learn from your past failures, you're at greater risk to repeat them. Although it's a sensitive topic, let's look at divorce as an example. Past research has found that in the U.S. 50% percent of first marriages, 67% of second, and 73% of third marriages end in divorce. You might wonder, what are the reasons for the progressive increase in divorce rates? The statistics are staggering. One common theory is that people enter their second or third marriages as a "rebound" and haven't allowed enough time to heal and set their priorities before saying "I Do" again. They tie the knot without learning why their last knot came undone. Therefore they are more likely to repeat their mistakes, resort to the same habits and another failed marriage ensues.

My purpose for using this example is to help you understand that if we don't learn from our mistakes, we waste the pain we experienced. That pain can be put to good use if you learn from it. As illustrated by Naomi's story, I believe that failure reveals at least three valuable lessons.

1. Failure reveals who your true friends are

Naomi's story is more like a math equation with subtractions and additions. On the road back home, her other daughter-in-law, Orpah, made the decision to turn back to Moab. Unlike Ruth who clung to Noami in the midst of their transition, Orpah took the easier road to a more familiar place in her past. The story goes that Naomi actually asked them to return to Moab (Ref. Ruth 1:8) since she didn't have any other sons to give them as husbands. But I view this scene as really a test of faith and friendship between these three ladies. Ruth was committed to Naomi and *her* God, regardless of where that path would ultimately lead them. She was committed to the *friendship*. Orpah was committed to the *function*, the role of being a daughter-in-law. But now that her husband was dead, she saw no reason to continue staying attached to Naomi—much less be mentored by her.

On that day, Naomi learned who loved her "for her," and not just what she could provide. I don't want to paint Orpah as a villain. Blaming her, or people like her isn't a healthy way to use our emotional energy. She's not malicious or cruel. She simply isn't a lifelong friend or somebody you can count on. You will learn who these people are whenever you go through a difficult time, or you're ducking from criticism. True friends will stick by your side, when it's popular and when it's not. True friends will associate with you when you're blessed and when you're broken, when you succeed and when you fail.

Failure acts as a "friend filter." When you're succeeding in life, everyone wants to be around you. But, when you fail, many of those so-called friends will disappear like Houdini.

In the moment, it hurts. You feel betrayed. But, true friends love you for who you are, not how successful you are.

Clearly, Naomi wasn't the jolliest person to be around. Her heart was heavy. She was mad at life and ambiguous towards God. She was a bit cold and unfriendly with the townspeople of Bethlehem. Not exactly the warmest personality. But mostly, it was her grief and bitterness talking and not the real her. Ruth knew that and still stuck by her side. She knew it was the aftershocks of a painful failure. Ruth knew this phase would pass. Real friends recognize that. After a failure, you learn whom you can trust with your heart.

2. Failure redefines your priorities

It took failure for Naomi to realize that living in Moab wasn't God's will for her life, and that her priorities were out of alignment. Hitting rock bottom forced her to re-evaluate the direction her life was taking. Although it seemed like a good idea at the time, moving to Moab was a mistake. It was a faithless decision. And faithless decisions always lead to dead ends.

But Jesus allows U-turns.

Better still, His grace rushes to our lowest points and awakens us to the path home, the road to restoration, the journey towards renewed values and spiritual wholeness. Early one morning, Naomi, *"arose with her daughters-in-law that she might return from the country of Moab, for she had heard in the country of Moab that the Lord had visited His people by giving them bread"* (Ruth 1:6). Naomi heard of God's faithfulness in Judah—how He was blessing His people. She must have thought, "What am I still doing here?"

It never ceases to amaze me how much dysfunction and pain people are willing to put up with before shifting their priorities back to God. Either because of pride or confusion, I've seen people extend their stays in the pitiful state of failure. They just don't want to admit they were wrong. They refuse to own up to their mistakes and repent. But the hidden gift of failure is being able to redefine your priorities and start over. If you can swallow your pride and admit that you were wrong, that you didn't have all the answers, that those people who warned you were actually right, you can save your future.

When you fail, you begin to redefine your priorities in life. You reorder the things that matter most to you. You look inwards. You look upwards. You take inventory of your life. This is a crucial step. After losing my house, I realized that "owning a home" had consumed me. I realized that although it's a good thing, it's not the greatest thing. I realized that putting my worth into material things was a mistake. I had forced a career upon myself (which I didn't enjoy) in order to make a certain amount of money, in order to pay for the house that I thought made me "successful."

Failure makes you redefine success.

It's good to own your house. But in my case, my house owned me. I had my house, but I was unhappy and not doing what I was really called to do. When things fell apart, I shuffled things around to make room for what was most important—my family and my ministry. God used my failure to push me into His presence, to trust His plan without trying to manipulate the situation. After a failure, it's an opportune time to shuffle your priorities back into order.

Redefine what your priorities are, and then revise your approach to support those priorities. This leads into my next point.

3. Failure revises your approach to life

Naomi chose not to waste her failure by channeling her pain into something positive—helping Ruth meet her kinsmen redeemer, her future husband, Boaz. Naomi found purpose and satisfaction in doing this. She drew from her depth of experience, knowledge and wisdom. She stopped feeling sorry for herself and quit trying to change her name to "Mara." Don't waste your failure. Instead, use it to revise your approach and avoid repeating the same mistake. Start by asking some of these questions:

- **What can I learn from this?** Take responsibility for what went wrong, even if it's not all your fault. You will never grow from failure if you make excuses or blame others. Look at things objectively and ask God to give you wisdom from your experience.

- **What could I have done differently?** It's been said that hindsight is 20/20. After the dust has settled and you accept responsibility, you then have the opportunity to analyze and ask yourself, what different steps could I have taken?

- **Do I need to acquire or improve some skills?** Sometimes our failures, especially in business, will reveal our lack of expertise or skill in a certain area. Those are opportunities to grow. You might consider making a self-development plan that includes furthering your education, acquiring certain licenses or credentials, or simply reading some books.

- **Who should I have listened to and why?** Identify the voices in your life that misguided you, so you'll know who to avoid asking for advice. On the flip side, acknowledge those God-fearing people who lovingly tried to warn you and get closer to them. Maybe it's a pastor, a parent or a wise friend.

- **What will I do next?** This might be the most important question. The only thing worst then failure is giving up. You must learn from your failure and press forward. Revisit your goals and try again. Earlier in this book I discussed the problems of staying stuck in your unseasons. Don't get settled in your history. Don't live in the past, but focus on the future. Don't dwell on who left you, but on who stayed. When you fail, at least fail forward!

Getting past your failure is not an easy process. Rebuilding takes time. Don't fool yourself. There is no spiritual magic wand that any preacher can wave over your life to bring instant completion to areas that have failed. Faith requires work. But the reason why I wrote this book was to inspire hope, to help you find God's purpose and power in your pain. And although failure is painful, it is not final. Every breath you take is a reminder that God isn't done with you yet. Whether your failure was a blunder or a catastrophe, your story isn't over. There is still time to turn things around because God is a God of new beginnings.

A SOFT PLACE TO LAND

I'm not going to lie. Few things scare me like the thought of making myself vulnerable by confessing my weaknesses. I shutter just typing that. Like most people, I struggle to open up about my faults for the fear of being judged or worse—rejected. And let's be honest. We all have a perception of ourselves that we want to protect. If you're in public ministry, the pressure to be perfect is ten times greater. We believe the notion that showing our weaknesses makes us "weak." We struggle to admit our failures because we don't want to tarnish our reputation or diminish our value. This mentality actually creates a culture of insecurity and superficiality that doesn't really help anyone, but instead turns the narrow gate of Christianity into a tightrope walk of religion. Secrecy breeds hypocrisy.

The word of God encourages us to practice vulnerability to form authentic community and care for each other. Two thousand years ago, James wrote, *"Confess your trespasses to one another, and pray for one another, that you may be healed. The effective, fervent prayer of a righteous man avails much"* (James 5:16). This Scripture makes a lot of people nervous—and rightly so. Who is eager to confess their shortcomings, to admit their failures? I'm certainly not. But James reveals that showing people your weaknesses and failures will bring healing. Vulnerability is an emotional risk that nightmares are made of. We cringe at the thought of opening ourselves up and exposing our faults. Satan plays on these fears like a stringed instrument. He convinces people to shove their faults behind closed doors and pretend that everything is fine. But everything is *not* fine. The further we isolate ourselves from the healing power of human connection and spiritual empathy, the deeper we sink into our shame.

The church is supposed to be a soft place to land, a safe environment to confide in others and know that they will pray for you. Notice I said, "supposed to be." I'm not naïve. I know that many have been hurt and betrayed by false brothers and sisters in the church. I know that the system is not foolproof. People may have let you down and instead of praying for you, they gossiped or treated you differently. However, I still believe that compared to all other communities and support groups, the church is still the softest and safest place to land. Yes, it's a flawed institution populated by flawed people. But I hold the opinion that every institution must be judged on the basis of its founder and its principles. Jesus founded the church. And He's the head of the church (Ref. Colossians 1:18). Scripture teaches that Jesus purchased our salvation with His precious blood (Ref. Ephesians 1:7). The church therefore belongs to Jesus and He loves us as His bride (Ref. Ephesians 5:25). Is the church perfect? No it's not. But it's still the safest place to find salvation and healing in a fallen world.

It's the second half of James 5:16 that gets quoted more often: "*The effective, fervent prayer of a righteous man avails much.*" We rehearse that line when we want our prayers answered. But before you start claiming your new house or spouse, in its context this truth is tightly tethered to the first half about confessing our faults and failures to one another. Confession is the catalyst of inner healing. When you face your fears and confess your struggles to godly, mature people, there is liberty. The pressure valve of anxiety is released. You feel lighter, even if your confession carries some consequences. Your small group at your church would be an ideal setting to open up. But if you can't find comfort there either, then you must connect with someone or a support group for accountability.

In conclusion, much of what we read in the Bible about failure is in the context of sin. But failure isn't always a sin. Sometimes we fail at attempting to do something right. In his time, Babe Ruth not only set the record for home runs in a single season, but he also led the league in strikeouts. Don't stop shooting for your dreams, because you're afraid to fail. As someone once said, "it's better to try and fail, then fail to try". We never learn the limits of our ability until we reach the point of failure. Thomas Edison tried over six thousand different types of light bulbs before he discovered the one that worked. His motivation to endure so many failures gave us the modern electric light.

Have you struck out lately? Keep swinging!

Has the light bulb not turned on yet? Keep trying!

Stand up and dust yourself off. Keep moving forward if it hurts. Hope again!

{Chapter 10}

The Struggle Israel

———————◆•◆•◆———————

E verything changed that day. I don't remember the exact date or even the year, but I'll never forget the time as a kid when one of my cousins ruined a favorite interest of mine. We were on a Sunday School field trip, sitting in our church van outside of Chuck E. Cheese's when he very causally told me, "Jacob, WWF wrestling isn't real."

Sorry for the false drama I just built up.

You were probably expecting a more serious story. But I sat there in complete disbelief. I thought to myself; *there's no way.*

Maybe you don't understand. Like so many boys who grew up in the eighties, I practically worshipped WWF (now called WWE). Here are some familiar names. "André the Giant."

"Macho Man" Randy Savage. "The Ultimate Warrior." "Jake the Snake" Roberts. Brutus "The Barber" Beefcake. And of course, "Hulk Hogan." I could go on and on. I had many of their figurine toys, their posters in my room and knew their signature wrestling moves. One time, I even got a chance to attend a live event with my dad and brothers. It was awesome; definitely a childhood highlight.

And I like millions of young boys who flexed their scrawny arms in the mirror and pretended to be the Hulk; I assumed it was all real – the storylines, the winners and losers, the pain and drama.

I debated with my cousin in the van that morning.

"It's fake," he said.

"No it's not. It's all real!" I argued with white knuckles and sheer defiance.

Well, needless to say, he was right. I didn't want to believe it. But I learned the truth. I had been duped! I still watched wrestling for a couple more years, but the charm was gone. Every time I watched with excitement, it would quickly vanish once I remembered, "the fight is fixed." It's all carefully scripted and choreographed.

After watching my older brother, Steven, wrestle in high school, I actually came to appreciate the real sport of wrestling. No glitz and glamour. No metal folding chairs slammed on someone's back. No jumping off any ropes. No face-paint and oiled biceps. Just two guys equally matched, pound-for-pound, maneuvering on the wrestling mat with strength, skill and endurance to pin their opponent. The sport of wrestling has been around for eons, but gained its legend in the ancient Greek Olympic games.

But there is one ancient wrestling match in particular that captures my attention and contains a profound lesson for those who are desperate for God and willing to change in order to possess their promises. It was nothing like the pro wrestling I watched as a kid or even the pure sport we witness in the Olympic games. This epic match-up was a fight for the ages, a clash between God and man, divinity and humanity, heaven and earth.

In Genesis chapter thirty-two, we come across the incredible story of Jacob wrestling with God. It was a grapple that lasted all night long. In fact, all his life Jacob had been wrestling and grabbing for significance. He wrestled with his twin brother Esau while they were still in their mother's womb. Then at birth, he came out grabbing his brother's heel, trying to get ahead. As a young man, Jacob dressed up in sheep's wool (pretending to be Esau) and he tricked his father into blessing him.

Jacob's life colorfully illustrates the ongoing conflict we have between *who we are* versus *who God calls us*. Like Jacob, maybe you are prone to disguise yourself in order to get what you want, such as acceptance, friendship or material things. But hear this: God will not bless the person you pretend to be. He will wait for you to own up to your life, to bury your past, to reveal your wounds, to face your failures, before bringing you into your destiny.

The turning point for Jacob came when he wrestled with God. For the first time in his life, he began to see himself through God's eyes. He started to recognize his own unique role in God's narrative. He stopped running from his past and finally started dealing with issues that hadn't been resolved for decades. His turning point wasn't pretty. It was gritty. It was a struggle. In the end, however, Jacob would hear God call him by a new name, one that marked his transition from schemer to dreamer.

POWER GRABS

The name Jacob means "heel-grabber." But for most of his life, he was grabbing the wrong heels, trying to position himself through scheming and manipulating situations, all while burning bridges with people along the way. He lived with a "what's in it for me" mentality. He was self-centered and "me-first" oriented. Now before you wag your finger at him with judgment, consider that most of us are just like Jacob to some degree. We are instinctively selfish. We are born thinking the world revolves around us. And society has led us to believe that the universe exists to make us happy and cater to our whims.

I would love to tell you that everyone comes to their senses on their eighteenth or twenty-first birthday, an epiphany of sorts, that *the world does not revolve around you*. But sadly, that isn't the case. Sadly, selfish kids become selfish husbands and wives, who then become selfish parents and so forth. This isn't a rebuke. It's a confession—one that I think we all can make. Let's be real. Who doesn't want to get ahead in life? Who doesn't want to "make it" or become somebody? Who would deny themselves a golden opportunity to be successful or strike it rich? Who would hand over their winning lottery ticket to a stranger? Most of us who see something we want or like are geared to take it. Ever since Adam took a bite out of that forbidden fruit, humans are wired to grab for what pleases the flesh.

That's a big problem.

If we allow that innate desire to control our lives we will stop at nothing and step on anyone to get there. Like Jacob, we will con and pose our way through life until we run out of people to hurt. That isn't the life that God designed for you. He created you for more than jumping from fix to fix.

To delve into Jacob's past and rummage through all his psychological baggage would require another book entirely. Whether it was grabbing his brother Esau's heel or conning him into trading his birthright for a bowl of soup, or whether it was posing as Esau to trick his father, Jacob was in a constant power struggle. His fixation on being first would eventually come back to haunt him. Life has a way of settling the score. For Jacob, that occurred when his father-in-law, Laban, tricked him into marrying Leah instead of Rachel—the true love of his life. He worked seven years for Rachel, but ended up with her sister. Whoops! The player got played.

Manipulation is the fruit of unbelief. People who manipulate to achieve success or gain influence don't really understand the origin of our blessings. God is the blesser. I don't think the word "blesser" appears in the Dictionary, but it most certainly describes our God. Every good gift and blessing flows from above. God is a good God. And He wants to show off His goodness in your life...your "real" life, not the one you're posing or distorting with manipulation. We can sabotage our own blessings by evading God's process and by refusing to acknowledge our desperate need for His presence. This is all building up to a cosmic clash between your will versus God's will, your pretense versus His purpose, and your image versus your identity.

When God encountered Jacob, he was about to reunite with his estranged brother Esau. Jacob was beyond nervous because He didn't know how his brother would receive him. Would he retaliate against Jacob and seek revenge for all the hurt he caused? Would emotions boil over? There were a lot of "what ifs." This state of vulnerability and desperation set the stage for an encounter with God.

I've spent considerable time in this book explaining how God heals our hurts and restores our hope, but now it's time for you to see the other side of God—the side of His grace that confronts us and afflicts us if necessary, teaching us how to lean on Him.

LIEUTENANT DAN MOMENTS

Most of us have seen Forrest Gump and watched the scene where Lieutenant Dan is strapped to the mast of the shrimp boat while the sea rages all around him. He's boiling with anger from the storm. Most of us can empathize with his emotion as he yells and challenges his maker for the unfairness that life has dealt him.

"You call this a storm?!" He screamed into the winds. *"It's time for a showdown. You and me. I'm right here. Come and get me!"*[2]

I can't repeat some of the other vulgar words Lt. Dan used. But what is portrayed is a man who is sick and tired of being *sick and tired,* who is ready for a no-holds-barred encounter with God. I actually like that scene because at least, even if a little edgy, this man is ready to face-off with God and come to terms with his faith.

Later in the movie, Lt. Dan and Forrest were on their boat

and he turns to Forrest and says, *"I never thanked you for saving my life."* He then smiled at Forrest, pulled himself out of his wheelchair and jumped into the sea for a swim—the same sea he once screamed in the middle of the storm. The camera zooms in on Lt. Dan and he smiles at peace in the waters. It was a pivotal moment for Lt. Dan because he finally found "himself" after a long period of disputing with God, disliking his life and his circumstances.

Minus the foul language, I think we all need to have our "Lieutenant Dan Moment" with God.

Jacob certainly did. The Bible says in Genesis 32:24, *" Then Jacob was left alone, and a Man wrestled with him until the breaking of day."* There's an aspect of this scene that often gets misunderstood. Jacob didn't start wrestling with God, but in fact, God started wrestling with him. This was the critical moment. Jacob is left alone, in the dark, facing what will probably be the fight of his life. In this kind of moment you would expect God to swoop in and comfort Jacob. But instead God shows up as an attacker. There are times that God will shake our world. He will disrupt our plans. He will delay our promises. He will do what is necessary to get our attention, provoking us to seek His face and pray with great fervency. God will grab ahold of you, until you grab ahold of Him.

God might be wrestling with you. And the pain you're feeling is not meant to destroy you, but to develop you—not to punish you, but to promote you. This isn't the WWF. It's not a sport or a game. This is real life—your life. God is using this book to ignite genuine hope in your life, a hope beyond your own devices or needs for control.

I want you to think about your life right now. What areas

hurt? Where are you struggling? Where is your faith being tested? What has you most frustrated right now? Consider this. God may be trying to provoke you to seek Him with greater passion and brokenness. He's waiting for you to let go of everything else and get a grip on His presence and say like Jacob, *"I will not let You go unless You bless me!"* You can't grab God with your worship and faith until you let go of people's opinions, until you let go of unhealthy comparisons, until you let go of frustration and worry, until you let go of distracting or toxic relationships. You can't grab God while still grabbing on to your past.

Let go and grab God.

He's allowing things to breakdown in your life so that you'll grope and yearn for His presence—until you find yourself like Jonah, crying out for mercy from the prayer room of a whale's belly.

How long will you run from God's call? How long will you deny the voice that's echoing greatness in your soul? When will you bury your ego and admit you need help?

How many times will you hit a dead end before you realize that God loves you enough to frustrate any plan that doesn't honor His purpose? How long will you make excuses for your disbelief or justify your quitting when the demands of life snowball?

You've heard the saying: *when the going gets tough, the tough get going.* Sometimes you have to fight for the things that matter. That's why God is confronting you. He wants to see your passiveness turn into passion; your intentions turn into actions, your complaining turn into praying, your faith turn into works, and your misery turn into ministry. He wants to turn your gripe into a holy grip.

Jacob had always been a grabber. And the same heel-grabbing personality that made him a liability was now an asset, because he funneled it heavenward. He was always a runner in life, but in the wrong directions. He was always driven, but for selfish ambition. God simply shifted his direction and used the same traits for his good. He does the same with us. He takes the traits that we think are bad or useless and redirects them for a holy purpose. But the transition from schemer to dreamer is painful.

THE BLESSINGS OF BROKENNESS

A couple chapters ago, I referenced the time I broke my foot while playing basketball. It was definitely a low point in my High School years, especially since it happened on the same day as try-outs. When I came down on my left foot, I felt a horrific snap that sent hot and painful shockwaves up my leg. I actually heard it pop. It sounded like a chopstick snapping in half. I was beyond bummed, not to mention embarrassed by the whole matter.

I couldn't say to friends and family that *I broke my foot after hitting a game-winning three-pointer from downtown.* Nope. No glorious stories to tell my future grandkids about my legendary broken foot. *Sorry kids, grandpa once broke his foot playing three-on-three hoops about twenty minutes before try-outs began. I never stepped foot on the court for an official game. Now, who's ready for some hot cocoa?*

There's actually a real point to this embarrassing story. And because I'm in a good mood, I'll tell you about my kindergarten incident. While trying to mimic the moves and kicks from the The Karate Kid movie, I lost my balance and landed awkwardly on my left arm. After screaming nonstop for about 30 minutes in the nurse's office, they determined that I probably broke a bone. Indeed. I broke my wrist and had to wear a cast on my arm. Okay, so what's the point of these stories?

You never forget your brokenness.

I can retell these stories with great precision and detail (more than what I wrote here). Many of my childhood memories are fond, but a little foggy, or remembered like Polaroid snapshots. But when I talk about my broken bones, I am immediately taken back to the time and place where it happened. I remember how I felt, what I said, what others said and the look of the doctors faces. I can put myself in those memories almost immediately. I'm sure you can do the same with your childhood memories— be it painful or pleasant.

The spiritual journey is no different. In the process of becoming who God wants you to be, there will be brokenness. When you endure a period of pain or crisis, you won't ever forget it. When you wrestle with God, His grace will mark your life in such a way that you'll never be the same again. Notice what happened with Jacob. We read in Genesis 32:25, *"Now when He saw that He did not prevail against him, He touched the socket of his hip; and the socket of Jacob's hip was out of joint as He wrestled with him."* As God wrestled with Jacob, God broke his hip. It's significant that God broke Jacob's hip because it's impossible to run on a broken hip.

Jacob had a pattern of running from his problems, running from his past, and from his calling. When you wrestle with God, He will break the leg (methods) you use to run back to your old ways, your self-dependency or manipulations. I would like to share with you the four blessings of brokenness.

1. Brokenness attracts the presence of God

David wrote, *"The sacrifices of God are a broken spirit, A broken and a contrite heart—These, O God, You will not despise"* (Psalm 51:17). Simply put, God is attracted to brokenness. Sincere worship flows unhindered from a broken and repentant heart; like the woman who broke her alabaster box and poured it on Jesus. The scent of her oils filled the room, but it was the fragrance of her brokenness that Jesus couldn't resist.

Believers often speak of wanting more of God in their lives. It's cliché. That sounds nice. But increasing your capacity for more of Jesus' presence will mean shrinking your capacity of self. John the Baptist summed it up: *"He must increase, but I must decrease"* (John 3:30). Brokenness prepares the way for a greater, more intimate encounter with God's presence. In that state, we are more in-tune with His voice, sensitive to His Spirit and patient with our surroundings.

Jacob's spirit was broken before his flesh was broken. His soul was bruised *before* his hip. Jacob would have never wrestled with God until he wrestled with himself and came to terms with life—his regrets, his weaknesses and his selfishness. Most people assume that brokenness can only be produced through plight and suffering—things that happen to us. But you don't need to wait for problems to show up in order to attract the presence of God. If you can learn to stay in a tender state through repentance and humility, you won't need to hit rock bottom or suffer, because you will already be broken.

Repentance and humility are the scented ingredients that

keep God's presence lingering in our lives. It's time to break your alabaster box, to present your body a living sacrifice—holy and acceptable to God (Ref. Romans 12:1). No longer should you be satisfied with maintaining the status quo in worship. Gone are the days of needing to be entertained or ordered to lift your hands in a church service. No more waiting for others to break the ice of praise and passion. Broken hearts are open hearts. And the more open your heart is, the more God will fill it—until your cup runs over.

2. Brokenness saves us from ourselves

Shepherds have been known to fracture the leg of a sheep that tends to stray from the flock—endangering itself to weather conditions and predators. Whether it's a young lamb's curiosity or a stubborn sheep determined to walk its own path, the pain of a broken leg will cause them to think twice before wandering away again. The sheep will associate drifting from the flock with acute pain. This is how God dealt with Jacob as they wrestled. And from time to time, it's how He deals with us.

Jesus, the Good Shepherd, breaks us to save us from ourselves. He'll touch you, so you can't run from His calling anymore. He'll break you so you'll walk with a spiritual limp, so your life will bear the marks of His mercy. Think of God as the ultimate equalizer. He comforts the afflicted and afflicts the comfortable. He exalts the humble and humbles the exalted. These expressions clue the dual nature of God in how He approaches our lives. Affliction is the other side of God's loving brushstroke. The Bible says, *"For whom the Lord loves He corrects"* (Proverbs 3:12).

Correction can be a painful process. But there's always a

lesson to be learned. I call this my *Fortune Cookie Theology*. When the shell of a fortune cookie is broken, you discover a positive written message inside. It hurts to be broken, but God always has a message, a purpose in your pain.

After breaking my foot, I was so bummed out. My hopes of playing hoops for my high school team were dashed before I could put on a jersey. But God had a plan. You see, at the time I broke my foot I was beginning to stray further from church. I was distracted from my calling. I wasn't focused on the things of God. Dangerous options lurked all around me—from drugs, girls and partying. I was walking on a tightrope. Then I broke my foot and it forced me to slow down and think about my life. Suddenly, I saw how far my heart had drifted—how close to the edge I was living.

Grace grabbed my soul and sat me down. During that period of time, I fell in love with Jesus all over again. I came to my senses. Mercy kept me from chasing the wind of empty promises. In the chambers of my brokenness, I rediscovered my passion and purpose to someday preach the Gospel.

Don't waste your pain! Seek the Lord and His direction for your life. What is God trying to tell you through your frustration? What dormant beliefs is He trying to awaken in your spirit? What dream is He trying to revive in this season of loneliness and desperation? That's where you will hear the still small voice of God.

3. Brokenness impacts the next generation

Your spiritual limp has implications beyond your life. Immediately after Jacob's wrestling match with God, the writer notated a Hebrew tradition, *"Therefore to this day the children of*

*Israel do not eat the muscle that shrank, which is on the hip socket,
because He touched the socket of Jacob's hip in the muscle that shrank"*
(Genesis 32:32). This custom is still practiced today. Orthodox
Jews don't feed from the area that God broke in Jacob. It
symbolized a place that didn't need to be broken or dealt with
again.

Here is the spiritual principle: what God breaks in you will
directly impact your family. The habits, sins and dysfunctions I
surrender to God in my life will drastically reduce, if not totally
eliminate, the chances of them reappearing in my children
or my children's children. But if I don't let God break me
(change me), the unbroken hip issues will show up in the next
generation. If you're a parent, you should want to pass down
your testimonies, victories, and blessings to your children—not
your vices, your anger, your pride or your addictions. In order
to prevent that from happening, God needs to work in you.
That's how oppressive cycles and family curses are broken.

It saddens me when parents don't see how their decisions,
big and small, will shape the future of their families. Jacob
became the father of Joseph, the dreamer who rose to prominence
in Egypt. Unlike his dad, Joseph didn't have to scheme or
manipulate his way to the top. He was a man of integrity. And
maybe his story would have never unfolded if his dad never
broke in the presence of God.

If you're a parent, your responsibility to your children goes
beyond providing them life's necessities. Hand down your
faith. Instill the Word of God in them and be the example. Show
them how to pray, how to give, how to serve the Lord.

4. Brokenness makes us more like Jesus

When God wrestled with Jacob, He was forming his new character and identity. As the match ended, Jacob wouldn't have a title belt to hoist up in the air, but rather a new name and a new limp. Anyone could look at Jacob from a distance and know that something had changed.

The fourth blessing and reason for brokenness is to ultimately form us into the image of the Son of God. In my opinion, this blessing is superior to any other byproduct of brokenness, because there is no greater purpose for us being alive than to become like Jesus Christ. God chose and saved you to make you more like Him. God is not interested in merely saving your soul, and keeping you out of hell, and taking you to heaven after you die. There is a deeper and wider purpose to the provision of salvation then avoiding hell. The Bible says, *"For whom He foreknew, He also predestined to be* conformed to the image of His Son, that He might be the firstborn among many brethren"* (Romans 8:29).

God predestined you not primarily to be saved, but to be conformed to the image of His Son. That's a great truth to celebrate. But before you high-five your neighbor or leap for joy, you must realize that the process of becoming like Jesus means drinking from the cup of suffering. No believer can become like Christ, or fulfill their life's mission, without afflictions. We read in Philippians 3:10, *"that I may know Him and the power of His resurrection, and the fellowship of His sufferings, being conformed to His death."* We typically zero in on the first part of this verse. But the second half of Paul's statement is equally essential. You can't experience greater fellowship with Jesus unless you're willing to suffer and carry a cross of brokenness.

I heard a story once about a silversmith who was once asked: *"How do you know when the impurities are burned away in the silver?"* He smiled and answered, *"When I can see my reflection in the silver."* Likewise, through a process of breaking and molding, God wants to see Himself in us. For Jacob, that meant transforming from "Jacob" to "Israel," a name that means "who prevails with God." Essentially, God was calling him to go from *pretender* to *prevailer*. The word prevailer isn't officially a word, but it makes my point.

It's time to prevail, to win in life—fair and square.

THE STRUGGLE CONTINUES...

As of right now, Instagram has over 2.4 million posts with the hashtag #TheStruggleIsReal. This hashtag is insanely popular. As you noticed from the chapter's title and heading above, I did some wordplay to highlight Jacob's struggle to become Israel— one "who prevails with God." But Jacob's transformation, even after the wrestling, was anything but neat and orderly. Jacob had a complicated relationship with God, but oddly enough it's one that we all can relate to.

Jacob's story reminds us that the goal of life is not perfection, but relationship—both vertically and horizontally. This chapter was mostly vertical—about you and God. In the next chapter, we'll focus on the hope of healing your horizontal relationships. And we're not done with Jacob yet. As we'll see, he had to take the opposite approach with his brother Esau. Less wrestling. More hugs.

Chapter 11

Hug the Cactus

———————◆•◆•◆———————

The entertainment industry appears to be a dog-eat-dog culture. And Hollywood is usually the last place to look for examples of grace and mercy. Most of us view Hollywood culture as heartless and superficial. Narcissism abounds. This is precisely why the following story is so unusual; it's the antithesis of what you'd expect from those in show business. Back in 2011, at the twenty-fifth Annual American Cinematheque Award Ceremony, a very un-Hollywood moment occurred on stage between two of its most well-known actors. Awarded the night's highest honors for "making a significant contribution to the art of the Moving

Picture," actor Robert Downey Jr. had the option of choosing who would present him with the prize.

He chose Mel Gibson.

It was a risky and bold move because Gibson's reputation had been severely tarnished, following a string of bad choices and public scandals. Gibson's downfall included a DUI in 2006, which made national headlines because of the actor's racist and anti-Semitic statements. Then in 2009, tabloids had a field day with Gibson's public infidelity and high-profile divorce, which was followed in 2010 when tapes were leaked online of an intoxicated Gibson demeaning his then-girlfriend with words that a human being should never be told. His once-golden image was now tainted, making him a public relations nightmare and a Hollywood outcast.

Now here Gibson was, one year removed from his last public ordeal, on stage to present a prestigious award to his longtime friend and former costar Robert Downey Jr. It was a tense and vulnerable moment for Gibson, one that most people would avoid. But Downey had a point to make. Although it was his moment to shine, his own checkered past wasn't too far in the rearview mirror.

Downey hadn't exactly been a model citizen either. His own fall from Hollywood graces fattened the wallets of the paparazzi and tabloids. The 1990s were brutal for Downey, who battled drug and alcohol addiction, public run-ins with the law and numerous relapses. Both his personal and professional life hit rock bottom; so much so, that filmmakers couldn't hire him even if they wanted to because insurance companies wouldn't underwrite productions with him on the cast. It was one closed door after another with not much hope. But Downey got a huge break when one Hollywood powerhouse took a high-stakes gamble on him when others avoided him like the plague. That powerhouse was none other than Mel Gibson.

When many assumed his career would never recover and his name would be permanently blacklisted, Gibson casted Downey in his 2003 film *The Singing Detective*—a decision that turned heads both in Hollywood and beyond. Gibson personally paid the colossal insurance premium as a way to help his friend climb back.

As it turns out, Downey never forgot that. Who would? Gibson was responsible for helping Downey revive a career and public image that was on life-support.

Fast-forward to this award ceremony as Downey sympathizes with Gibson—who is now the one in need of a helping hand, of forgiveness, of reconciliation with colleagues that had all but dismissed him. When Downey took the stage and accepted the award from Gibson, he seized his moment and caught the Hollywood elitists and fans by surprise. Here are his words:

> Actually, I asked Mel to present this award to me for a reason, because when I couldn't get sober, he told me not to give up hope, and he urged me to find my faith—didn't have to be his or anyone else's as long as it was rooted in forgiveness. And I couldn't get hired, so he cast me in the lead of a movie that was actually developed for him. And he kept a roof over my head, and he kept food on the table. And most importantly, he said that if I accepted responsibility for my wrongdoings, and if I embraced that part of

my soul that was ugly—"hugging the cactus" he calls it—he said that if I "hugged the cactus" long enough, I'd become a man of some humility and that my life would take on new meaning. And I did, and it worked. All he asked in return was that someday I help the next guy in some small way. It's reasonable to assume that at the time he didn't imagine the next guy would be him. Or that someday was tonight.

So anyway, on this special occasion...I humbly ask that you join me—unless you are completely without sin (in which case you picked the wrong... industry)—in forgiving my friend his trespasses, offering him the same clean slate you gave me, and allowing him to continue his great and ongoing contribution to our collective art without shame. He's hugged the cactus long enough. [And then they hug.] [3]

Mel Gibson stood in the background appearing to be just as surprised by the short speech as everyone else. This moment seemed to mark a turning point for Gibson, who has since begun to reclaim his career and produce films again. Now, I understand these men aren't saints. As a disclaimer, I don't recommend we start looking to Hollywood for moral direction. Clearly, we need to base our lives on the Word of God. But Downey used a fitting metaphor that described the often complicated, painful process of embracing your weaknesses and forgiving difficult people—something he heard Gibson say. He called it *hugging the cactus.*

I'm not sure who exactly originated the phrase, but I think

it gives us a clear mental picture of how to approach our pain or those who cause it. This metaphor can certainly depict our acceptance of our innate weaknesses and shortcomings, but I'm particularly focused in how it depicts our complicated relationships.

We all have cactus people to hug.

Cactus people like Gibson or Downey may not deserve a second chance, but neither did we. I think that's the point of it all. Those are the lenses we should be looking through.

WE ARE CACTUSES

In my opinion, a cactus person is anyone you have offended or that has offended you. A cactus relationship is one that is emotionally strained or torn. It can also be those painful relationships that you're stuck in—like a family member, neighbor, or co-worker. These are people who poke at you, but for reasons beyond your control, you can't simply run away. You have to find a solution where you are and make it work.

I've hugged a few cactuses. How about you?

I've got a couple more to go. You?

It's not fun.

Jacob's cactus was named Esau—his fraternal twin. And their long-awaited reunion recorded in Genesis chapter thirty-three reveals the delicate process of reconciliation. Their *hugging the cactus* moment was dramatic and tense.

Of course, this time Jacob was a different man. And he had a limp to remind him. But his brother Esau, the one he conned and hurt years ago, had also changed. Both men had grown up and had time to smooth out the rough edges around their characters. Much time had passed—time to think, time to repent, time to evolve. But time doesn't fix everything and heal all wounds, which is what made their reunion long overdue. There was still a lot of unfinished business between the two. Each brother had his reason for avoiding the other. Each had his side of the story.

We all have our *sides of the story*. And it's always the *right* side. We're always the victims—never at fault, never culpable. Our version of events is the *only* version. We force people to take sides. Anyone who doesn't take our side, well, obviously they're not smart or spiritual enough to discern who is really to blame. Clearly we played no part in this family feud, this Christmas blow-up, this nasty breakup, this petty catfight, this High School drama of he-said/she-said, this frenzy of Facebook blocking and unfriending. We were just minding our own business when a cactus person poked us.

Pardon all the sarcasm.

Aside from bullying (which is a real problem), it usually takes two to tango. You can't hug a cactus until you realize you're a cactus in some ways, too. Those who struggle the most with forgiving others are usually those who haven't come to terms with their own need for forgiveness.

Let me come out and say that I've read dozens of books and heard countless sermons on "forgiving others" and in most cases, all the focus is on what the other person did to you. We spend all our efforts dismantling and theorizing why the other person did what they did and how it makes us feel. Rarely do we discuss the part we must own in the story. Seldom do we address the needles that protrude from within ourselves and may have agitated (if not, instigated) the conflict. We shift blame. We dodge responsibility. We *plead the fifth* about our own thorns. Thanks to Adam, it's our human nature. When questioned by God about his disobedience, he conveniently threw his wife Eve under the bus without a blink of hesitation. The world's population at that time was 2. Our blue planet is now home to a cozy 7.4 billion. That's a lot of buses.

You can't hug another cactus until you first hug your own. I know that message doesn't sell. It stings. It pokes. But unless we get honest about our thorns, can't expect our broken relationships to heal or improve. We have to swallow our pride and work on becoming the best version of ourselves through the power of the Holy Spirit.

To hug your thorns isn't some form of religious shaming and self-degradation. It's simply being truthful about the ways in which your character, habits or tendencies is frustrating your relationships and pushing people further away.

We'll never completely remove all the needles from our lives. But that doesn't mean we should give up on the process of becoming who God has called us to be. In the meantime, hug your cactus first. Confess your faults. Own your part. Face the side of you that hurts, that's scared, that's dark. Because usually what's hurting you will hurt others.

We are all cactuses. And yet that didn't stop Jesus from hugging us.

God's love hugged you in your most thorny condition—a lost sinner without a shred of hope. You could say, "For God so *hugged* the world, that He gave..." And when He hugged your cactus and all your thorns, He took them upon Himself. He wore them as a crown.

As Jesus hung on the cross, our thorns pricked and pierced

his mind. He absorbed the barbed wires of sorrow and sin. And it wasn't just the thorns that ripped His flesh; it was the nails in His hands and feet, the thirty-nine lashes on His back, the spear in His side, the jagged surface of the cross digging into fresh wounds. Jesus didn't just hug the cactus; He became one. A Savior without sin became sin for us that we might inherit eternal life.

Then, in the fray of agony and bloodthirsty mobs yelling "Crucify!", Jesus does the unexpected. With every ounce of fading strength, Jesus prayed aloud, *"Father, forgive them, for they do not know what they do"* (Luke 23:34). The universe gasped. The heavens hushed. The mobs stood bewildered. Forgiveness reached a depth it had never known, by embracing cactuses like us.

If Jesus forgave you, then you can forgive others.

If Jesus could hug you, then you can hug others.

If you'll obey God's command to forgive, you'll see that even cactuses grow flowers.

Jesus saw the flower on your cactus, the beauty in the broken, the grace in the disgraced.

How could Jacob and Esau hug each other after years of estrangement and hurt? How could they reconcile their differences? I suggest because each brother dealt with the cactuses in their own hearts. Especially in Jacob's case, he was forced to face his inner thorns when he wrestled the angel. He couldn't be reconciled with others until He first reconciled with God. Jacob couldn't hug a cactus named Esau until he hugged a cactus named Jacob. He realized that although him and his brother were different, they both had thorns.

What I've said might not make the process of healing a

relationship easier, but it will make it better. I want you to gain an understanding of life that few stop to consider—usually because they're so busy being upset and bitter.

THE EVOLUTION OF BITTERNESS

Satan's agenda is to perpetuate ignorance. If he can keep you in the dark, then he can keep you in bondage. But the Holy Spirit illuminates truth. This isn't merely psychological warfare; this is spiritual warfare. Every action or thought you carry out should be guided by the Holy Spirit and based on the Word of God. Otherwise you're only shadow boxing and not actually punching out the problem.

Let's see how bitterness evolves and how to prevent its roots from deepening in your life.

1. Wrong produces Hurt

Hurts happen when someone directly or indirectly wrongs you. The wrong can be verbal, physical or even psychological in nature. It's safe to say we have all been wronged at one point or another. No one is exempt because, again, we live in a fallen world populated with flawed people. Wrongs will happen on a daily basis. The nature of the wrong will vary from circumstance to circumstance. The level of hurt will vary from person to person, based on how severe the wrong was and what provoked it.

It helps to remember that injustice is not only a product of this fallen world, but is often engineered by Satan – the accuser of the brethren (Ref. Rev. 12:10). But we are reminded in Isaiah 54:17 that, *"No weapon formed against you shall prosper…"*

Whenever you're wronged, keep that scripture in mind. It doesn't mean that weapons won't form. They *will* form against you. But they *won't* prosper because you're a child of the living God.

2. Hurt produces Anger

If a hurt isn't healed properly, it will lead to anger and vengeance. Anger isn't necessarily a sin. Sometimes it's the appropriate response. God's grace allows us to be angry for a period of time, but eventually that anger has to convert into something constructive.

Ephesians 4:26 crystalizes this point: *"Be angry, and do not sin: do not let the sun go down on your wrath."* I'll be the first to admit; this is easier said than done. But when anger festers, we quickly start to justify our retaliation. The Bible reminds us that it's not our job to settle the score. Romans 12:19 states, *"Beloved, do not avenge yourselves, but rather give place to wrath; for it is written, "Vengeance is Mine, I will repay," says the Lord."*

3. Anger produces Bitterness

If anger consumes the heart, it will eventually germinate into a root of bitterness. This is when you permanently accommodate your hurts. At this point, people generally stop sympathizing with you and expect you to find closure and move on with your life. Friends and family won't come around as often because your personality is soured with negativity. Cynicism will begin to taint your perspective of life and even God. Eventually, you blame everyone who doesn't agree with you. You can try to cover your bitterness with deceitful acts of diplomacy, but in the end you won't feel any better about yourself. Your blame games will corner you into a stalemate situation where nobody wins. The moment you perceive that the other side is winning or you feel threatened; you'll try to manipulate family members and friends by maintaining the status of a victim. You may even attempt to manipulate Scriptures and God's Name in order to rationalize your bitterness or convince neutral parties to join your side.

Sadly, you'll get to the point where you don't even like yourself. Regardless of who was originally right or wrong, your hatred will invert until you can't stand your own reflection. Bitter people usually end up bitter with themselves more than anyone else. You become your worst enemy.

Let me take it a step further. Your injury can become idolatry—if you listen to it, cradle it, enshrine it and see the world through it. You bow to its demands. You let it control your emotions.

If you're involved in ministry, read the following lines carefully. Any ministry conceived in anger or hurt will either be stillborn or self-detonate with vanity. Since victims need attention, your ministry will end up being a public therapy session where you are either the star attraction that needs praise, or a voluntary scapegoat that needs pity. Ministering "through" pain is different than ministering "for" pain. Therefore, allow God's grace to hide you, heal you and help you forgive.

If you're bitter, you cannot enjoy God's blessings because you won't allow yourself to. You won't embrace new things because your mind will always rehearse the past. You won't welcome new relationships because you'll be afraid that this new person might do you wrong like others have. You won't trust God to the fullest because part of you will blame God for what happened, or feel that God is punishing you for not trying harder.

If you're bitter, you won't love serving people because you'll feel that others owe you an apology and should actually be serving you instead. You'll struggle to give because you'll always be the one taking. If you're bitter, you won't be happy because you keep defining happiness based on how you feel from day to day, instead of by God's grace and love. I once saw a quote that read, "Bitterness is letting someone live rent-free in your head." Well, if that's the case, I say it's time to evict that emotion and change the locks!

MENDING OR ENDING?

Maybe there is someone from your past or present that boils your blood with anger or freezes it with fear—a relationship conflict that turns your heart into a furnace or an igloo. Whether tensions need to cool or worries need to thaw, relationships don't fix themselves. It requires time and effort on both sides. If you're the only one trying to mend the relationship, you're going to burn yourself out. People are not machines we can tinker with. If the other party isn't willing to contribute to the healing process, it's going to be a very frustrating experience.

You first need to decide if the relationship is worth fixing. Hear me out on this. Because every moment you spend trying to mend a torn relationship is a moment stolen from a whole relationship. There are only so many hours in a day, days in a week, weeks in a month, and before you know it, you've worn yourself out trying to pump life into an expired relationship. Of course, this doesn't necessarily mean you should give up.

Everyone deserves a second chance. You simply must decide whether that second chance is with you; whether it's in your best interest to restore that relationship. We're commanded to love our enemies, not to live with them.

Forgiveness is not an option, but friendship is. Certain relationships could cost you your destiny. Not all relationships are worth keeping if they lead you backwards or divert your spiritual growth.

Some people will never change.

Some will never grow up.

Not because they can't; because they won't.

Depending on who this person is, the circumstances, and what relation they are to you, you must to decide whether you need to fight for the relationship or let it go. This decision won't be easy. In a book about hope, you'd think I'd be more optimistic about all of our relationships. To a degree, I am. God can do miracles in relationships. I've seen it. I've felt it. But relationships often take a life of their own and can become very complicated. After you forgive someone, it really comes down to personal choice whether a friendship continues.

My views on relationships might be radical. Maybe it's due to my own experiences. Maybe because I'm getting older and realizing that I don't want to spend the next half of my life nursing old relationships, or anything, that isn't relevant to my calling as a husband, father and pastor. Not that I'm scratching out people who don't benefit me, but rather, I'm selective about who I let into my life. There are certain people I have to love from a distance.

Some relationships require more maintenance than others, and that's perfectly fine so long as it's the right relationship.

Even healthy relationships require upkeep and safe boundaries. You can't give up on crucial relationships because they demand your time and effort. Relationships take work, especially the closest ones—the ones you can't afford to lose.

But I digress.

Nearly twenty years had passed since Jacob stole Esau's birthright. Only thin shreds remained from the fabric of their family. These twins were more like strangers than brothers. Yet the thought of each other opened a flood of memories. Years split apart couldn't silence the echoes of regret—over how stories got spun, over *who* took *whose* side, over business left unfinished. No doubt, these men were different men now. Esau wasn't the same huntsman who traded his inheritance for a sip of soup. Most notably, Jacob wasn't the same manipulator who tricked his father. He was now a humble hobbler in search of God's promises. Both brothers had grown up and grown out of their old rivalry. But that growth was about to be put to the test.

The day came—the day that almost never happened. After two decades, Jacob and Esau would finally come face to face.[4] It's daybreak and the sun crouches on the horizon like a tiger on its prey. That's how Jacob felt the morning he limped along and lifted his gaze towards Esau in the distance—who apparently liked to travel with a large entourage, four hundred men to be exact. But it was too late to back out. Plus, Esau might have been nervous, too. I'm speculating of course, but anyone who needs that amount of security around him is a little paranoid.

When the two brothers met, it didn't live up to the hype. No fists thrown. No insults hurled. No scores settled. What happened must have taken everyone by surprise. Instead of brawling, there was bowing. Instead of hitting, there was hugging. No kicks, just kisses. It was, by all accounts, a loving reunion of two brothers who shared a complicated past but decided to let things go. Not what you would expect after so many years of silence. And yet this scene captures the hope of broken relationships in way that few do in the pages of scripture. But these men didn't get there by accident, or by waiting around for a spontaneous turn of events. They both, especially Jacob, took measures to end their feud and hug the cactus.

You don't need to squint at this story to spot its golden lessons, enlarged by two characters who each braved the risks and left their respective comfort zones. Insecurities were unshelled the moment they locked eyes and didn't turn back, shrinking the gap of disaffection with every step. They were ready to listen, to move beyond just a cease fire, to bury the past and be a family again—even if things weren't picture perfect.

There is hope for your relationships. It's just about setting the right expectations and taking things in stride. When repairing a relationship, focus on progress not perfection.

Jacob humbled himself. So should we.

Jacob blessed, not cursed. So should we.

Esau focused on the present, not the past. So should we.

Jacob and Esau hugged the cactus. So should we.

{Chapter 12}

Halfway is Not Enough

A bout 350 years ago, a shipload of colonists landed on the northeast coast of America. The first year they established a town. The next year they elected a town government. In the third year, the government wanted to build a road five miles westward into the wilderness. Then in the fourth year, the townspeople attempted to impeach their new government because they all thought it was a waste of time and money to build a road five miles westward into unknown territory. Their rationale was: *"Who needs to go there anyway?"*

The same group of people who braved 3,000 miles of treacherous ocean, storms, and distress were now unable to see five miles out of town. In a matter of a few short years, they had lost their pioneering spirit and vision. They settled on the coasts where they docked, not realizing the vast frontier of unclaimed territory just beyond the western horizon. After all those miles, the truth was, they had only reached the halfway point in a land filled with promise.

Frontiers left undiscovered.

Sights left unseen.

Potential left unfulfilled.

It can happen to us, too.

The only thing that scares me more than failing, is settling. Most times when I fail it's because I'm trying something new or different and didn't see the results I hoped for. But settling is the curse of not ever knowing what could have been; it's that looming sense of regret after you held back, shied away or played it too safe.

For the things that you value most in life, almost doesn't count. Halfway isn't far enough. As the saying goes, *"almost only counts in horseshoes and hand-grenades."* In the game of Horseshoes, points are scored by how close your horseshoe lands to the stake. Technically, you could win the game without ever hitting the target. And as for hand-grenades, proximity will usually do the job. But in life, we rarely get credit for almost and halfway. In eternity, there are no "almosts."

Almost didn't count for King Agrippa. Despite Paul's compelling testimony, Agrippa could not be fully persuaded to become a Christian.

Almost didn't count for Terah, who was Abraham's father. Terah had the potential to etch his legacy in the annals of Biblical patriarchs, but instead serves as a cautionary tale of settling halfway. Abraham is considered the father of faith by both Christians and Jews, but it may surprise you that Terah *could have* been a father of faith had he only finished his journey. I know that's a bold opinion. But if you read the story, you'll see that the pilgrimage from Ur of the Chaldeans to the land of Canaan actually started with Terah, not Abraham.

Genesis 11:31 reads, *"And Terah took his son Abram and his grandson Lot, the son of Haran, and his daughter-in-law Sarai, his son Abram's wife, and they went out with them from Ur of the Chaldeans to go to the land of Canaan; and they came to Haran and dwelt there."* It was Terah who took the first step towards a land of promise that flowed with milk and honey. But something happened along the way. He settled and died at the halfway point, in the land of Haran. Terah never reached his destination. He never saw the land that would come to symbolize the promise of God.

TRAPPED IN TRANSITION

"Whoever finishes a revolution only halfway, digs his own grave."
- Georg Büchner

Too often, people start off on the right track towards their calling, but get stuck somewhere in transition. It is not the will of God for you to settle for partial promises and halfway victories. God is calling you to finish what you started. But like Terah, we may get distracted by emotions or issues from the past. Terah was called to Canaan, but instead settled in a place called Haran, which oddly enough, was a place named after his late son "Haran." The Bible tells us, *"Haran died before his father Terah in his native land, in Ur of the Chaldeans"* (Genesis 11:28).

Next thing we know, Terah *"...came to Haran and dwelt there"* (verse 31).

It seems to me that Terah settled in a place that reminded him of his past—a wound that never healed, an issue that was never resolved. It seems emblematic that Terah couldn't move beyond Haran—the same name of his son who died too young. I wonder how often we do the same thing? How often do we start off strong, but then get trapped in transition? In a previous chapter, I wrote about the problem of being stuck in an expired season of life. But in this case, Terah illustrates how we can move in the right direction of faith, take the right people and have every intention of reaching a new reality, only to hit a road block from the past. Terah's past ultimately defined his future and broke his stride. Verse 32 says, *"...Terah died in Haran."*

Everything was going according to plan until Terah's caravan set up camp in Haran. Something changed. It was like an invisible rope from the past had tied itself to his heart and wouldn't stretch another centimeter. Maybe Abram tried to convince his dad to keep moving, rather than settle down in that place. If so, it was met with a glassy expression of inattention. He lost his desire to finish the course.

Terah's sail had lost his wind.

But when your sail loses its wind, you paddle.

You keep going. You keep trusting. You persevere.

You cannot become who God has called you to be while living in yesterday. What invisible ropes are keeping you from entering your Promised Land? What emotions or fears are derailing you? What regrets are you still holding on to? We can't get trapped in transition and never obtain the future we're called to. If you're following a God-given dream, *don't look back.*

Settling halfway to your dreams is almost as tragic as never dreaming to begin with. Maybe that sounds a bit harsh. But for Terah, and anyone who seeks to do God's will, halfway is not enough.

Sort of…isn't.

Almost…doesn't count.

Don't get me wrong. God isn't requiring us to be perfect, but obedient. There's a big difference. Some think it's impossible to be obedient, which isn't true. It's impossible to be perfect. I also think we should celebrate progress and not downplay baby steps—so long as we don't become stagnate. That's really the issue here. No matter where you are in your journey towards your hopes and dreams, keep moving forward. Don't give up. Don't abandon hope. There is a solemn utterance of destiny calling you to let go of the past and embark on the road less traveled. It's the whisper of the Holy Spirit saying, *"you will seek Me and find Me,* when you search for Me with all your heart"* (Jeremiah 29:13).

Halfway to anything special or significant is usually the hardest phase in the process. It rings true for me as a writer. Every time I start writing a new book, including the one you're holding, there is a tidal wave of adrenaline and determination in the first few chapters. During those first chapters, I feel like Marco Polo on the open seas. But then about midway through my manuscript, the sail loses its wind. It's called *writer's block.* I can only explain this as a mental funk, a creative drought, like four flat tires on a stock racing car, like a baker with no eggs and butter. You get the point. Writers block is where books can live or die.

About the middle of every manuscript is when the temptation to quit is the strongest. For every book I finish writing, there's been a least two or three that fizzled halfway through (sometimes earlier). Life is much the same. We can get trapped in transition, stuck at the halfway point to fulfilling our dream.

The only way I've been able to overcome writer's block is to...keep writing. Now, of course, there are some helpful techniques that writers can use to help find their creative flow again. But none of those techniques will write the second half of my book for me. At some point, I need to start typing again.

At some point, you need to get back to doing whatever God called you to do, or rekindled the passion to finish what you started.

UNFINISHED BUSINESS

In the summer of 2015, I was blessed with the opportunity to travel with my wife Cherie and a team of youth to Barcelona, Spain for a mission trip. It was our first time visiting Europe, one that we'll never forget. Not only did we get to make new friends and minister to the Apostolic churches in Spain, but we got a chance to view some amazing architecture throughout the historic city.

In preparation for our trip, I did a little research on some of the places we could visit. One site in particular caught my eye. It was the historic Sagrada Família church. This famous Roman Catholic church building, which broke ground in 1882, is one of the most beautiful and prestigious structures in the world—let alone Spain. The dream of renowned architect Antoni Gaudí, this nature-inspired work of art attracts millions of visitors every year. It is by all accounts an architectural masterpiece.

There's just one little problem.

The building has never been completed.

After 133 years, the Sagrada Família is still a work in progress – with an estimated completion date of 2026. Keep your calendar open!

Gaudi worked on the church for forty years, and even devoted his last fifteen years exclusively to it, but he died in 1926 before it was finished. Since then, the project has been in a constant state of flux, with a number of different architects and builders, but it has yet to be opened or used as a church. It's beautiful, but not functional; unique, but unusable; started, but never finished.

In many ways, life can be like the Sagrada Família. We all have started something that we never finished. Oh, yes, we intend to. We're getting around to it. We're working up the courage to. It's in our plans. It will get done, *eventually*.

Unfinished things clutter up our lives. The half-mowed lawn. The letter started but never sent. The abandoned diet. The degree we never finished. The phone calls never returned. But it can be much more serious than that: unresolved relationships, unpaid debts, unforgiven people, unhealed emotions, unconfessed sins, unkept promises, unfulfilled dreams, and the list goes on.

We can go through life leaving behind a trail of unfinished business and unfulfilled dreams.

God didn't call you to go halfway! He didn't heal you so that you could settle for less. He didn't give you a second chance so that you would forfeit the second half of your life. We worship a God who finishes what He starts. As Paul said, *"being confident of this very thing, that He who has begun a good work in you will complete it* until the day of Jesus Christ" (Philippians 1:6)

Recently I learned that the artist and sculptor Michelangelo is credited with creating forty-four statues. However, he only finished fourteen. In fact, there's an Italian museum dedicated to his unfinished works—massive chunks of marble with only a hand or a leg finished.

Don't let that be how your story ends.

God doesn't call us to start strong, as much as He calls us to finish strong. Not to say that *starting* isn't a big deal. You can't finish until you start. But I believe there are many who have already started and are somewhere in-between; in-between who you used to be and who you're becoming, frustrated because you wish you were further along than you are or stuck in spiritual survival mode.

The challenge for many believers is not whether they know they're called by God, but whether they're *still called*. I will presume you've heard God's call in your life. The question is, have you responded?

As believers, we usually associate the words "calling" or "call" with ministry. But truly, God could be calling you to do some unfinished business in areas that aren't related to public ministry at all.

Maybe your marriage started strong, but after five or ten years you started drifting apart because you hit some bumps in the road. Now, you're wondering if it's too late to save your marriage. It feels like you're falling out of love and it would be easier to walk away, rather than to stay and work it out. You have unfinished business.

Maybe you're still hurt and upset with a friend who betrayed your trust, broke a promise or insulted you. Yet, he or she might feel hurt about something you did in return. Either way, the two of you have successfully avoided each other or continue to pretend things are okay, when deep inside you know something is wrong. You have unfinished business.

Maybe your dream is on life-support and you're wondering if there's still hope – even after failing, after being rejected, after quitting too early. You live in the shadow of greatness and yearn for a second chance to prove yourself to God and to those who believe in you. Your worst fear is to die knowing you never took a risk and tried again. You have unfinished business.

There are numerous scenarios that could describe your situation and what must be accomplished in your lifetime.

What has God called you to do?

What assignment has your name on it?

Where do you need to hope again?

The goal of life should not be to coast until the rapture or until we die. While on this earth, there is plenty to do and live for. There are some finish lines that must be crossed before you cross into eternity. You have to live every day, every moment, like it's your last.

There's a man in scripture we don't know much about. His name is Zerubbabel. Under the rule of Cyrus, he was granted permission to return to Jerusalem and rebuild the temple. He successfully laid the foundation, but then construction halted for seventeen years. People teased him and said, *"The hands of Zerubbabel have laid the foundation of this temple; His hands shall also finish it. Then you will know that the Lord of hosts has sent Me to you."* (Zechariah 4:9). God is not a halfway God. If He gave you the courage to start, He'll give you the power to finish. God is the author and *finisher* of our faith.

GOD DOES *NOT* MEET US HALFWAY

Have you ever heard the phrase *"God will meet you halfway"*? I admit to saying this on more than one occasion—with only the best intentions, of course. On the surface it seems like a harmless belief. However, I've given this idea more consideration and have put it under Biblical scrutiny. I've come to the realization that God actually does *not* meet us halfway. Allow me to explain.

The logic behind this phrase is that if we can only reach the halfway point in God, He will meet us there and make up the difference. Again, it sounds harmless. But it imposes a notion that isn't supported by scripture nor fits in the narrative of the Gospel. Take for example, the doctrine of salvation. The reality is, God came to earth and was manifested in flesh as Jesus Christ, precisely *because* our righteous efforts could not sufficiently atone for sin and reach the heights of God's glory. God didn't meet us halfway at Calvary; He came all the way. Salvation is not the combination of God's 50% plus our 50%. Salvation was completely and totally God's achievement. He came all the way from where He was to where we are, so He could be in a relationship with us.

Then, He waits for us to come "all the way" to Him.

God gave us 100% of Himself.

He wants 100% from us.

100% love.

100% obedience.

100% of your heart and mind.

I've been happily married to my wife, Cherie, for 15 years. You don't stay married that long, or longer, by only meeting each other halfway. Building a lasting marriage will require more than 50% from each spouse, but 100%. Many couples land in divorce court because they were waiting for the other spouse to meet them in the middle. True love cannot be measured by adding up half and half, 50-50. Inevitably, there are circumstances that will call for you to give 100% and receive nothing in return. The same is true for your spouse. Only this kind of commitment will carry your marriage through the ups and downs.

For the things that matter most in life, halfway is just not enough.

God never met Terah at Haran. And that's why, not long after, God spoke to Terah's son Abram: *"Get out of your country, from your family and from your father's house, to a land that I will show you"* (Genesis 12:1). God wanted a finisher, someone who was willing to break away from halfway-minded people.

The calling was clear but painful. The Lord didn't just want Abram to relocate, but to leave his father behind. Terah's name means "delayed." I can't think of a more fitting characterization of his life. Terah was stuck in delay and died without ever reaching his destination. In order for Abram to avoid repeating his father's mistake, he had to detach himself from people who were content with halfway, people who lived in the past. The same rule applies to us.

Are there any "Terahs" in your life?

Is someone or something delaying your calling?

Don't assume you can settle halfway and that God will meet you there. Hidden in the word "call" is the word "all." Your call requires all. You'll never fully realize your potential in Christ until you surrender all to Him.

BLIND OBEDIENCE

In the eleventh century, King Henry III of Bavaria grew tired of court life and the pressures of being a monarch. He made an application to Prior Richard at a local monastery, asking to be accepted as a contemplative and spend the rest of his life in the monastery.

"Your Majesty," said Prior Richard, *"do you understand that the pledge here is one of obedience? That will be hard because you have been a king."*

"I understand," said Henry. *"The rest of my life I will be obedient to you, as Christ leads you."*

"Then I will tell you what to do," said Prior Richard. *"Go back to your throne and serve faithfully in the place where God has put you."*

When King Henry died, a statement was written: "The King learned to rule by being obedient."

If only we were as willing as King Henry to obey what God has called us to. Too often we are more afraid of obedience then we are of disobedience. We humans find the concept of blind and complete obedience disturbing because it pushes against our sensibilities and demands that we give up our autonomy. But when we place our trust in Jesus, it's because we know that His ways are higher than ours and that He sees the end from the beginning. He leads us in the direction of completion and maturity.

The Bible says, *"Therefore, leaving the discussion of the elementary principles of Christ, let us go on to perfection..."* (Hebrews 6:1). Here, the word "perfection" in the Greek is "teleiotes," which denotes "maturity." It comes from a root Greek word "telos," which means to make perfect, to carry through completely, to accomplish, to finish.

Did you catch that?

God is calling you unto His definition of Christian perfection—to mature and finish what was started, by His grace and through His power. Friend, your destiny is not an unattainable goal. You don't have to be perfect to obey, but obedience will lead you to maturity, to accomplishing what God has called you to do.

The perfection that God seeks in you is not *flawlessness*, but of *faithfulness*.

Godly obedience actually sets us free from perfectionism (by the world's standards) because Jesus would never command us to do something without providing the capacity to do it. He would never set a goal you couldn't reach, a finish line you couldn't cross. He would never place unrealistic demands on your life. Yet, God is looking for faithful obedience. "Blind" obedience is not mindless and robotic adherence; it's God's taking you by the hand and causing you to triumph.

By faith, Noah obeyed God's command to build an ark without any evidence of rain. From start to finish, Noah's act of blind obedience took 43,800 days. But…he finished.

By faith, Abraham obeyed God's command to leave the land of familiarity behind for a place he had never seen before. There were bumps in the road. But…he finished.

By faith, Paul obeyed the call of God and abandoned his former life in order to preach the Gospel. He endured numerous setbacks and hardships that nearly killed him. But…he said, *"I have finished the race."*

Jesus obeyed the sovereign will of God in the garden of

Gethsemane with the words *"Not my will, but yours be done."* He endured the pain, shame, and brutality of the crucifixion. But… in the end He uttered, *"it is finished."*

It's not how you start; it's how you finish.

{Chapter 13}

Your Destiny is Calling

F orget about the past, forget about what's happening right now, and just peer into the future. Dreams that were overshadowed by pains from the past are now free to fly in the light of God's grace. Aspirations that were once drowning in the waters of emotional hurt and despair are now alive above the waterline. Potential that was once walled in by fears and tears, setbacks and struggles, now has every opportunity to flourish.

Look in the mirror and see that you're a different person. Look at your eyes; you're wiser. Look at your smile; you're happier. Look at yourself; you're free. Everything that the past kept you from seeing, and the enemy kept you from being, is before you today. Every opportunity that was closed because of your past is now open.

You are free to hope again.

The ghosts of past failures and flaws can be cruel. Even if you are freed and healed, you might still hear the chatter of doubt and fear. They know they've been healed, but the struggle comes with moving forward. Moving forward can be difficult when you've spent a lifetime cradling your hurts and caressing your regrets.

Some people are so used to living with a particular problem that, once delivered from it, they sometimes end up in the same situation again, because they don't move into the future. The key to staying free is in finding purpose for your life.

Themes from the Book of Ruth are peppered throughout this book, and for good reason. The life lessons and analogies you can draw are endless. I would like to put on my spiritual scuba gear and dive deeper into Ruth's decision to follow Naomi into Bethlehem. Having experienced so much loss, she came to a new season of hope that would not only change her life but her legacy.

LEAVE IT BEHIND

Following Naomi's footsteps, Ruth embarked on a journey that would change her life forever. With her back toward Moab, each step she took was one step closer to her destiny. Life had not treated Ruth very well. In fact, it was quite painful and dark. Let's review some of her troubles: her husband died, her father-in-law and brother-in-law also died, her mother-in-law was an emotional train wreck, her own family was not in the picture;

all that she had ever dreamed about crumbled before her eyes. Her life was far from peaceful, nowhere near normal.

With a bleeding heart and a weight of uncertainty, Ruth clung to a destiny she could faintly hear through the noise of life. Her soul clung to a dream. She held on to the garments of a woman whose future seemed no brighter than her own.

She willingly left her homeland on nothing more than a *hope* and a *hunch* that life would get better. No promise, no guarantee, no evidence that she wouldn't fall back into the same hole. The only way to walk away from your past is by having faith that where you're headed is far greater than where you've been.

It takes an extraordinary faith to leave all that you know but, more so, to cling to something that is unstable. Naomi was unstable. She was in no condition to lead. She was caught up in a whirlwind of emotions. Ruth's sister-in-law, Orpah, was just as unstable because of her own experiences. Yet Ruth had enough sense to know that anywhere was better than where she was. One thing was certain: she was going to leave her past in the past.

Faith doesn't require a degree in theology or a vast knowledge of the Bible. It doesn't require knowing the right people, having the right position, or being in the right mood. Faith demands one thing—*risk*. Will you risk embarrassment, failure, or rejection? No risk, no reward.

What would have happened to Ruth if she had stayed in Moab? What would have come of her? It would have been utter tragedy. But only when you say "goodbye" to your past can you say "hello" to your future. Don't stay stuck in Moab. Don't linger in the same dimension of life where you started. Many people are not willing to cut ties with the past, perhaps because part of her still wants to live in the past.

Don't fear the future. God has not given you a spirit of fear but a spirit of love and power, and a sound mind.

Orpah's fears crippled her progress. Her struggle over whether to stay back or move forward illustrates a profound contrast with Ruth. Both women were at the same place in life. Both had lost their husbands. Both had deep wounds and tattered hearts. Both faced the same dilemma, the same crossroad. Sharing the same mother-in-law, Naomi, they began the journey with her toward Bethlehem. However, one major difference surfaced between Ruth and Orpah. Ruth left Moab with reckless abandon. Orpah left with reservations, still torn between two places.

Even though Orpah was journeying out of Moab, she still had Moab in her heart. Frankly, no matter where she went, her past would be with her. As the story goes, Naomi, Ruth, and Orpah had an emotional collision. Naomi urged these young ladies to return home. Telling them that she had nothing to offer, they wept together.

As tears filled their eyes, Ruth and Orpah took different paths. Ruth would press forward, even in the shadow of uncertainty. Orpah would turn back toward a dismal past. Perhaps she felt there was something in her past that she couldn't live without. Perhaps the fear of failure blinded her vision of the future. Either way, Orpah headed back to the place she needed to leave. Orpah represents those who have the opportunity to leave their pasts behind, but don't. Ruth represents those who seize the opportunity and won't look back.

THE POWER OF MOVING FORWARD

After the somber scene had ended, the long walk toward Bethlehem continued. This time there were only two women. As Ruth clung to Naomi, soaking her shoulder with tears, her mind was made up. She made a vow that would change her life forever. What a powerful example of moving forward despite your circumstances! Ruth had what every person needs: determination. She was determined to start a new life in a new place. She was determined to hope again; to live again. Leaving Moab was just the beginning. Destiny was calling her to something far greater than she could have imagined. Maybe you see yourself in the position of Ruth and Orpah. Maybe you're stuck at the crossroads of destiny, contemplating which direction to take.

While living in the past, you can harbor excuses, feel sorry for yourself, and live like a victim. To move to the future, you have to make personal sacrifices and enter unknown territory. Ruth illustrates the power of determination and the will to live a greater life. The following are some principles I think Ruth would advise anyone in her situation.

1. Move forward in the face of your flaws

When Ruth made the decision to go to Bethlehem, she was still hurting, still tender from the great losses in her life. But moving forward is part of the healing process. As Ruth walked the long road to Bethlehem, her heart was being mended. Everything wasn't perfect and many questions still lingered. But she didn't let her flaws and failures keep her from attaining what she believed she could have.

191

You cannot wait for perfect conditions before you move forward. That day is never going to come. As long as you keep waiting for the right time, right day, and right situation, you'll never accomplish your goals. Now is the time to act. Yesterday is over. Tomorrow isn't guaranteed. Today is your greatest opportunity to move your life in the right direction. Ruth was missing pieces. Her heart was out of tune. She was under construction, with much work to be done. However, that did not stop her from moving forward. The fact is, the missing pieces could be found only by going to Bethlehem. She wouldn't be fully restored until she moved there. Oftentimes, your *prescription* is in the *process*.

You might be looking at yourself and thinking that you aren't quite ready to pursue your dreams and fulfill your destiny. You might be thinking that you aren't prepared to hope again. You might see yourself too far gone, too undone, too afraid, too timid, too broken, too inexperienced, too weak, too poor, or too powerless to move forward. Don't listen to the lies of the devil! He's trying to keep you down. He's afraid of you. He's afraid of God's purpose in your life.

God isn't looking for flawlessness, but for faith.

2. Move forward in the face of your feelings

Orpah's decision was an emotional one. Her feelings dictated the path of her life. With swinging emotions and gushing tears, she allowed her feelings to guide her at the most important crossroad. Her emotions blurred her vision, causing her to lose sight of the future. Feelings are unpredictable and unreliable. They can change from one day to the next.

Ruth had feelings, too. However, she didn't let her feelings drag her back to Moab. Was she emotional? Yes. Did she cry? Yes. But her heart yearned for a better place.

Feelings are like a thermometer; they change with the climate of circumstances. But they can't be trusted. The Bible tells us in Jeremiah 17:9, *"The heart is deceitful above all things, and desperately wicked; Who can know it?"*

I'm sure there have been times when you didn't *feel* like doing something, but did it anyway. Perhaps you didn't feel like forgiving a friend for offending you. Perhaps you didn't feel like praising God when you were going through heartache and pain. Maybe you didn't really feel like going back to school to get your degree. Maybe you didn't feel like breaking off that toxic relationship. To trust your feelings alone in these sorts of decisions can get you in trouble.

Emotions are not necessarily evil, but use them wisely.

To go where God is taking you, you have to put your feelings aside and trust His will. To go where He wants to lead you, you must learn to conquer your emotions. There is a time and a place for feelings. To move forward, you need to see with the eyes of faith. Ruth's emotions were overflowing. But feelings aren't enough to take you to your destination. Just look at Orpah. Her emotions were overflowing as well, but she allowed them to pull her back. She made a decision based solely on how she felt. Ruth, in contrast, clung to her destiny with faith.

3. Move forward in the face of your fears
Nothing about Ruth's vow to move forward was comfortable or reassuring. The brush of fear and the winds of uncertainty surrounded her path. All that she had known and experienced was miles behind her. Migrating to a foreign land with

different customs, people and philosophies was a huge leap of faith. Although her steps were hopeful, she had no tangible assurances. There were no guarantees that she wouldn't be rejected or, worse yet, deported. There were no guarantees that she would survive. With a bitter mother-in-law for a guide, and a trail of tears behind her, she embarked into the mystery of God's will.

Fear is something we all face. No one, no matter how spiritual or knowledgeable, can escape the reality of fear. To be faced with fear doesn't mean you're a failure or spiritually dysfunctional. Contrary to what many teach, fear is *not* the opposite equivalent of faith. Some teach that to have fear is *not* to have faith. But without fear, faith isn't faith at all; it's simply an action. Without fear, there's no need for courage, no need for bravery. Faith is the human response in the midst of fear.

Don't stop moving forward because you're afraid of the odds. Don't give up on your road to destiny because fear follows in your tracks. Don't turn back because the future frightens you. You've come too far to turn back now. God has done too much for you to retreat.

In order to move forward, you must overcome your personal fears. Whatever your fear may be, it can chain you to blocks of normalcy, keeping you from possessing the great things God desires to give you. Second Timothy 1:7 states, *"For God has not given us the spirit of fear, but of power, and of love, and of a sound mind."* The word *fear* in this passage is derived from the Greek word *phobas*, which means, "running scared." In other words, God has not given us the spirit of *running scared*. Many think that they cannot move until their fear is gone. That's not the message God is sending.

His message is that you *must* move in spite of your fear.

The only way to overcome fear is to face it. Facing your fears is not erasing them; it's making a decision to proceed regardless of their existence. This will stretch your faith.

HANDFULS OF PURPOSE

And let fall also some of the handfuls of purpose for her, and leave them, that she may glean them, and rebuke her not.
(Ruth 2:16, KJV)

Once Ruth became a citizen of Bethlehem, she quickly realized that getting there was just the beginning. She survived the journey. She pressed past her flaws, pressed through her feelings, and prevailed over her fears. She finally arrived at her destination. Moab was only a memory and Orpah was long gone. She now stood on the soil of new beginnings, where God called her to be. But now what? What's next?

Ruth knew her *place*, but not her *purpose*. She knew that Bethlehem was home; but beyond that, she had no real idea of her purpose. It's possible to be at the right place in life, and not know your purpose. A fitting example is knowing you're at the right church, but not knowing what it is you're supposed to do. Or, knowing you're in the right place financially, physically, or spiritually, but clueless about your destiny. Ruth had done so well to this point, yet she lacked one key ingredient — *purpose*. She had *position* with Naomi and a *place* in Bethlehem. All she needed was a true sense of *purpose*.

In the second chapter of Ruth, you'll see that she discovered her destiny in a most unexpected way, by doing what any ordinary person would do. Since Naomi couldn't help much, Ruth headed off to work. At dawn each day, Ruth arose and joined groups of needy people in gleaning the fields for food. In those days, the poor were allowed to comb the fields and gather food the scraps left behind by the harvesters. These were leftover, flawed vegetation that fell along the way.

The field owner, Boaz, noticed Ruth and ordered his servants to leave handfuls of food on purpose. He wanted to make sure that she received something good. So Ruth began to pick up those scraps, not realizing that Boaz was caring for her. The story of Ruth and Boaz turns to a fairy-tale-like romance authored by God Himself. But it began with handfuls of purpose. It began with little signs that indicated something greater was about to happen.

If you look closely around you, you'll discover some handfuls, some indicators that God has you where you are for a purpose. You'll discover His hand at work in your life.

The handfuls of wheat were only a fraction of what Boaz had for Ruth. The same is true for you. God has so much to give you. Like Boaz, not only is He wealthy, but He is looking for an opportunity to bless you.

Look at what the Bible says: *"Then Boaz said to Ruth, 'You will listen, my daughter, will you not? Do not go to glean in another field, nor go from here, but stay close by my young women. Let your eyes be on the field which they reap, and go after them. Have I not commanded the young men not to touch you? And when you are thirsty, go to the vessels and drink from what the young men have drawn.'"* (Ruth 2:8, 9) In providing for Ruth, Boaz satisfied one crucial area in her life—*hunger*. Boaz was able to command his harvesters to drop wheat on purpose. This showed not only that the famine was over, but that the crops had exceeded expectations. God had openly blessed His people with bread.

Ruth was starving on the inside, as you may be. She was hungry for healing, for happiness, and for a better life. God wants you to know that the famine in your life is over, and that He has so much to give you. What the famine has stolen from your heart, your family, your relationships, and your dreams, the Bread of Life is going to replenish. What the famine has drained, God is going to refill.

Those who sow in tears shall reap in joy. You've sown many tears. You've planted some pain in the soil of life. Now it's time to receive your return; your harvest is here!

Enduring struggles and making it to this point hasn't been easy, but the tide has turned and God is going to bless you. That's why God allowed you to be emptied. If He hadn't, you wouldn't be able to receive what He has for you now. Ruth picked up *handfuls* of provision because her hands and heart were empty.

The wheat of God's goodness is coming back to your life. Doors that were shut are going to be opened. Void spaces in your heart are going to be filled. If you were thinking about giving up or throwing in the towel, think again. To abandon what God has for you right now is to commit spiritual suicide. Recognize His handfuls of provision; they're all around you, waiting for you to grab ahold of. God has so much wealth— His fields are abundant. He has enough power, resources, and grace to sustain you. His will is that His fields become your fields, whatever belongs to Him belongs to you. As Boaz left handfuls for Ruth, hoping to capture her heart, God is leaving handfuls of provision and purpose, so that you will become completely His.

What benefit is there to spending a lifetime making excuses? Orpah went back to Moab because Moab was still *in* her, and she wouldn't separate from it. She missed her moment. But Ruth saw beyond her flaws, feelings, and fears. She heard something that is also quietly calling you—the call of destiny, the call to hope again.

Do you hear the call?

Do you hear God whispering your name?

Can you recognize the handfuls of purpose?

You were hurt, but not destroyed; rejected, but not forsaken; down, but not out. Life hasn't been easy. But here you are. Your heart is still beating. Take hold of your future and dare to hope again. Dream with your eyes open!

ACKNOWLEDGEMENTS

I'm grateful for my amazing wife, Cherie, and my children, Makai and Chloe. You inspire me to hope again. Thank you! Dad and mom, thank you for always believing in me and showing me how to endure for God's glory. Thank you, CityLight Church, for supporting my ministry and allowing me to be your pastor. Thank you, National Messengers of Peace, for inspiring me to impact this generation for Christ. And lastly, thank you to everyone who has ever rejected or hurt me; because in the words of Joseph, *"you meant evil against me; but God meant it for good."*

ABOUT THE AUTHOR

JACOB RODRIGUEZ is the founder and lead pastor of CityLight Church in Mountain View, CA, in the heart of the Silicon Valley. He is the president of the National Messengers of Peace, an international ministry that reaches more than twenty thousand young adults. Jacob also holds a Bachelor of Arts degree in Theology and has authored several books including *Shift* and *Lying Lions*. He and his wife, Cherie, have two young children, Makai and Chloe.

Twitter: @JacobRod
Facebook: @PastorJacobRodriguez
Instagram: @JacobRod29

NOTES

(Endnotes)

1   Grace period. (2017, January 31). In Wikipedia, The Free Encyclopedia. Retrieved 18:52, April 19, 2017, from https://en.wikipedia.org/w/index.php?title=Grace_period&oldid=762851706

2   Zemeckis, R., Tisch, S., Finerman, W., Starkey, S., Roth, E., Burgess, D., In Schmidt, A., ... Paramount Pictures Corporation. (2001). Forrest Gump. Hollywood, CA: Paramount Pictures.

3   [The Telegraph]. (2011, October 18). *Robert Downey Jr asks forgiveness for Mel Gibson.* [Video File]. Retreived from https://youtu.be/_AAJuynxnTQ.

4   This narrative is found in Genesis chapters 32 and 33.

Made in the USA
San Bernardino, CA
30 May 2017